T0349449

THE SOUL OF THE DEAL

DAY ONE TO EXIT

Creative frameworks for *buying, selling,* and *investing* in any business

MARC H. MORGENSTERN

RODIN BOOKS™

Rodin Books 2022

**RODIN
BOOKS™**

Hardcover ISBN 978-1-957588-08-7

eBook ISBN 978-1-957588-09-4

PUBLISHED BY RODIN BOOKS INC.
666 Old Country Road
Suite 510
Garden City, New York 11530

www.rodinbooks.com

Book and cover design by Alexia Garaventa

Manufactured in the United States of America

For my Dad, Stanley W. Morgenstern (aka, Boppie).

Generous and beloved mentor to his household,
civic, and chosen families

CONTENTS

AUTHOR'S NOTE

All stories are genuine but made faceless for privacy and confidentiality reasons by combining transactions as a composite or by changing name, gender, industry, geography, financial data, or other easily identifiable clues to the actual individuals or circumstances. A special thanks to Bob Hurwitz (Founder of OfficeMax) who gave permission to be quoted and discussed.

Every deal involved numerous people who collectively negotiated and architected separate pieces and parts of transactions. Human nature being what it is, we all experienced them differently and recall each deal (and our own role and contribution) primarily through our own eyes.

When transactions produce superb outcomes, every participant vividly remembers playing a pivotal (almost outcome-determinative) role in the deal theater, probably the *lead*.

When things end poorly, the same person (in the same deal) recollects they were merely an *extra* in the play; or maybe even less than that (an *understudy* who never appeared on stage and had no responsibility for the consequences).

"Success has many Parents. Only failure is an orphan."

The most acute deal observation of all time is anonymous. Wish I'd said it.

FOREWORD

Long before founding OfficeMax, the company I ran (Professional Housewares Distributors) was making our first acquisition. Marc was the young attorney assigned by a partner to represent me. We worked intensively through challenging circumstances and closed. Without Marc's savvy guidance the deal wouldn't have happened. That was the first time, but not the last.

Since then, I've done dozens of high-stakes, big money deals with Marc over many decades; startups like OfficeMax (he was the Founding Lawyer) and raising money from billionaires and venture funds to fuel corporate growth, acquisitions, and exits.

His expertise and emotional intelligence are world-class, and his humility authentic.

I've worked with him as a pragmatic but visionary advisor, lawyer, co-investor, entrepreneur, mentor, partner, and friend. He's invested in my businesses, and I've invested in his.

Marc's negotiating style is unlike anyone I've ever worked with, at once collaborative, creative, and innovative—always seeking to understand the emotional needs, wants, and desires of all parties while focusing on the facts and business objectives.

His vision and insight let him facilitate successful outcomes when all parties might have otherwise talked past each other.

No matter how difficult or tense the issue, his tone is always constructive and never confrontational. He sees and listens with the eyes and ear of a musician, communicates clearly, cuts to the heart of issues, and does all of this with deep understanding of business, financial, operational, and legal context.

Sometimes I think he has a sixth sense when it comes to planning deal tactics and strategies, but he also instinctively reacts to new information as it's being presented and processes it into the transaction.

Marc establishes trust with all parties, negotiates unique structures reflecting unique facts, and closes intense and time-compressed deals quickly.

He's also an incredible teacher, musician, and pianist!

I think it's great he's willing to share his wisdom and experience with others through his Maxims and his stories. Here are two of my favorite things I've learned from him:

> *An Expectation Unarticulated is a Disappointment Guaranteed.*
>
> *Structure unexamined is Stricture.*

This book is a huge bargain and must read for everyone in what he calls the DealCircle© (business buyers and sellers, entrepreneurs, investors, lawyers, accountants, management). It sets the stage for everyone to take a needed step back, see things from the viewpoints of others, and achieve more than they otherwise could in selling and negotiating their way through life and deals.

Odds are good you'll also laugh a lot. Not a bad combination.

Bob Hurwitz

Chair, BioMendics
Founder, OfficeMax

INTRODUCTION,
OR *SHAKEDOWN STREETS*
AND BEATS

My foundational lessons for negotiating and structuring billions of dollars of complex business deals (from formation to exits and IPOs) came from,

- Selling encyclopedias door to door in rural areas in Ohio and West Virginia as a teenager, and
- Following the Grateful Dead (while majoring in foosball and playing keyboards in my rock band during college).

More or less what you expected. Right?

No?

Encyclopedia selling taught me the building blocks of sales *and* negotiating. Door-to-door selling is all real-time, face-to-face. Sell (or don't sell) right now to *these* people in *this* house. There is no pay for try. There are no dress rehearsals. The pressure is relentless and it's always showtime.

Perfect negotiating training.

The Grateful Dead's jam band style provided a master class in the dynamics (and benefits) of active listening and real-time improvising. Call and response. An adaptive system. Behind every spontaneous riff was deep domain knowledge, empathy, soul, and a lifetime of gigging out and practice.

More perfect negotiating training.

Learnings from these informal tutoring environments were augmented through more than 400 corporate buying, selling, and financing transactions from Silicon Valley to Shanghai, and from OfficeMax to co-founding Within3, virtually a 360-degree view of the deal world.

Fuse those experiences together and you emerge with a negotiating style premised on flexible jam band philosophy, engaged listening to respond (not rebut), and persuading (not bludgeoning). Win what you need, mindful that you don't need to win everything you can see. A "Dealjammer."

In the first chapter you'll pound streets with me armed only with rudimentary, unrefined encyclopedia-selling tactics.

In later chapters, you'll meet the Seller who thought my CEO was a Messenger from God, and the overly optimistic promoter who predicted the stock we were buying was going to be worth either fifty dollars or fifty cents.

We'll discuss how Einstein's Theory of Relativity impacts closing transactions, how to spot black swans before you see them, and why the Grateful Dead are America's musical venture capitalists.

The goal?

This book is strongly about people and emotion. ***People are the epicenter of every deal.*** The heart and soul of the deal.

Understanding humans (what drives them to act, react, or not act), is the essence of selling and negotiating and leads to tactics and strategy. Not the other way around.

Deal structures change. People don't.

Hopefully aspiring Dealjammers can experience these authentic stories as if they were at the origin gig, see the secret scenes behind the stage curtain, and access the otherwise inaccessible. Not *what* happened in the deal so much as *why* and the process of *how* it happened.

A central theme is the concept, consequences, and reality of a "DealCircle"—the totality of stakeholders and decision-makers potentially impacting any negotiation.

Some participants are intuitively obvious: buyers, sellers, investors, management, directors, lawyers, and deal intermediaries. Some not so much (customers, suppliers, the unemployable uncle, government agencies).

Every individual person in the DealCircle (DealCirclers) can help your deal if they choose. They can also hurt your deal through indifference, inaction, or intent. Cross purposes abound. At the nucleus of each Deal *eco*system lies a pervasive human *ego*system requiring endless transactional tending.

A second major theme, applicable to almost every business sale transaction, is: ***The Seller's Mantra is Certainty and Confidentiality.***

Like most "Morgenstern's Maxims," the phrase is a short-hand *principle* to capture (as well as facilitate) thinking. They're not *rules* to memorize and mechanically apply. (I'm not good at following rules.)

In an increasingly hard and digital universe, soft human skills like empathy, humor, and perceptive listening (combined with persuasive storytelling, substantive knowledge, emotional intelligence, and flexibility) will be more important than ever to anchor your deals.

I exited every Grateful Dead concert happier than entering. Hope you feel the same when you reach my "Outroduction."

MHM

Cleveland, Ohio
2022

CHAPTER 1

LESSONS FROM AN ENCYCLOPEDIA SALESMAN

Door-to-door encyclopedia sellers are seriously unpopular and yet some are remarkably effective at selling encyclopedias. They know how to engage, negotiate, and close with a customer. Others don't and quickly quit.

My education as a dealmaker began innocently enough the high school summer vacation I responded to this ad:

> *Unique opportunity for the right individual. Unlimited compensation! Are you a real self-starter and closer? Our best personnel make $500/week. Call 216.xxx.xxxx to come in for an interview.*

They didn't say what the job was and I didn't care. They had me at $500. That Universal Encyclopedia Company sure knew what they were doing!

Daily morning classes with veteran encyclopedia sellers were laced with practical know-how and personal stories and anecdotes. I still remember some of the stories.

Formal (almost academic) high-powered training materials supplemented our sales training. Strong building blocks of domain expertise for future use in selling or negotiating.

The hardest universal lesson for me to accept I heard in the classroom but only fully learned and appreciated later on the road. Without real world context, I *listened* but didn't *hear*.

Most people make decisions about buying some "thing" (or buying into an "idea") *emotionally* long before they justify the decision *analytically*. This concept was completely counterintuitive to me.

In selling encyclopedias you painted a picture, you told a story illustrating their value. You appealed to people's hearts before you appealed to their minds. Perception and persuasion. That's the right sequence and approach in any discussion or negotiation.

If you can get your counterparty emotionally committed to a transaction, obstacles to a Closing disappear. In "The Boxer" Paul Simon worded it this way: from that moment on "a man hears what he wants to hear and disregards the rest." The archetypal definition of confirmation bias. Intellectual and emotional blinders.

Counterparties will rationalize and "*under*hear" (and ignore) unfavorable/adverse terms (or fact-specific risks) regardless of actual negative economic consequences and will "*over*hear" (and overvalue) rewards and positive facts. The combination skews a dispassionate risk-reward deal analysis in favor of the emotional decision.

At a personal level, whether I'm on the buy-side or sell-side, I'm least effective negotiating when forgetting to achieve emotional buy-in *before* launching into my analytical economic value propositions.

Odds of selling an encyclopedia are 100-1 against

Late each day (after morning classes followed by a several-hour car ride) we'd be dropped off at 6:00 p.m. on the same street corner where we'd be picked up later that night at precisely 8:45. (Mobile phones would have made this much easier!)

It was only a few days into this gig before realizing that if any member of my crew (veteran or newbie) knocked on one hundred doors, almost none would open. No one was home, or someone *was* home but unwilling to engage with you.

If you were invited into six homes, five "no's" were almost guaranteed, and routinely all six. I'm optimistic by nature (any glass I see is on the verge of overflowing) but even I had to concede that this was clearly bad news.

There were inherent challenges to sales success. High among them were that residents weren't typically eating dinner at home and saying to each other:

Homeowner: "Gosh, I really hope someone drops by unexpectedly tonight to sell us an expensive encyclopedia."

At *best* turndowns were at super loud volumes and laced with bad words.

Homeowner: "Whatever [barnyard epithet] you're selling, we don't want any, you %$#@!"

At *worst* people threw things at you (some of which were sharp), threatened you, or called the police. Not infrequently all three.

Girl Scout cookie sellers on the other hand received significantly warmer greetings and were welcomed into most of those same homes.

Same "Whatever you're selling, we absolutely
Homeowner: want to buy some. Come on in."

Given a choice I might have joined the Girl Scouts but barriers were obvious, so I stuck with encyclopedias.

Things got easier when I became able to sympathize with a few of the people who yelled at me. (Not so much the ones who *threw* things at me!) From their perspective I was an unknown, uninvited intruder into their personal space, spurring annoyance and maybe fear. Yelling was their outlet.

In response I made a conscious choice not to hear the words as being *about* me (even though they were aimed in my direction). The pejorative language and decibel level weren't personal to me as an individual. Both were just "noise," not "signal."

And I also reluctantly accepted that most people wouldn't treat me as kindly as my parents. With lowered expectations disappointment was less frequent.

Rejection is unpleasant but unlikely to kill you

Remind me. What was the good news about receiving verbal abuse through an open door?

Consider the alternative. What were the chances of making a sale if I were knocking on a closed door talking to myself? Charm is wholly ineffective against wood. No sale.

On the other hand, any time someone came to a door to say "No" was an interaction that *could* lead to a sale. An angry and dismissive "no" wasn't ideal but it was better than no engagement.

My response tended to be making a joke to soften their reaction and get them to laugh *with* me or *at* me. I didn't care which. Humor is a great social lubricant. Disarms people and dissipates tension.

If they still didn't open the door (but I could see them through the window) I would hold up a beautiful, colorful picture from the encyclopedia to attract their attention; hopefully leading to an invitation to enter the house.

I always believed I was only a "yes" away from success.

What kept me pounding pavements was straightforward. We got paid $76.50 for each encyclopedia we sold. We got paid *nothing* without a sale. Coming close wasn't rewarded. Door-to-door selling isn't horseshoes; you don't score a point (or get paid) for landing within six inches of the stake.

There was no compensation for time spent walking or knocking; only for selling. Results were rewarded. Process wasn't.

Motivation and determination to sell are necessary (but not sufficient) to make a sale. Engagement with an audience (someone to sell to) and perseverance are still required. My Dad often observed that you could be the best neurosurgeon in the world, but if you didn't have a brain to surge on, it didn't matter.

For pragmatic reasons sales presentations occurred only in a *home* with wife and husband present. If only one spouse was home, we politely said "hello," thanked them for their time, and moved to the next house. We eliminated wasted, unproductive time that would reduce the number of pitches we could make that evening. Encyclopedia selling is a classic game of large numbers.

Why?

> **INDUSTRY TIP:** Single people don't buy encyclopedias and neither do apartment renters.

If we made a presentation to either husband or wife by themselves (and their response was positive) an explanation inevitably followed that they couldn't give us a check until their spouse approved the purchase.

The first "yes" (without the second "yes") *felt* like a sale but wasn't. Money wasn't going to change hands until an unseen decision-maker, an unseen stakeholder in the outcome, agreed.

If we were in a house with a couple, we had the right setting and both decision-makers (all the stakeholders); everything needed to immediately close a sale.

We needed a "yes" from one decision-maker, and either a "yes" (or anything other than a "no") from the other. Silence from the second spouse was interpreted liberally as a "yes."

Being physically close before and during the presentation definitely helped. As soon as you entered the house you intentionally invoked all five of your senses to familiarize yourself with everything you could about this customer.

I could *smell* a customer's dinner cooking. Through the inevitable smoky haze, I could *see* and *taste* their cigarette brand of choice. I could *hear* which TV channel or radio station they were tuned to.

Digital cookies weren't necessary to track their purchasing preferences.

What You Saw	**How You Responded**
Manchester United mug	Talk soccer, not baseball
Beatles records	Talk rock music, not Beethoven

Sports and music are universal unifying languages. You'd quickly (and safely) find common human connections and be chatting away like old friends long before raising topics like purchasing an encyclopedia. Visiting behavior. Building trust and establishing rapport. Key deal skills.

Talking religion or politics wasn't encouraged. High risk, emotionally volatile topics where sharp disagreements were more than likely and could kill a sale before you even started selling.

Exposure to the importance and power of close physical observation should have prevented the following embarrassing exchange which occurred years later with my "CEO-Seller-client" after an in-person negotiating session.

CEO-Seller:	"It was really helpful that I got a good look at my counterparty's watch and shoes. He's a real peacock. Gives me tremendous insight into how to deal and appeal to him based on what he values and displays."
My shocked response:	"I've never looked at anybody's watches or shoes (female or male). No one could conceivably attach the level of importance you're ascribing to them."
CEO's even *more* shocked response:	"Marc, are you kidding me? You're wearing a Grateful Dead watch and a Grateful Dead belt plus black running shoes with an orange stripe in a business conference room where everyone else is wearing a $20,000 Rolex watch, a navy-blue suit, and black-tie shoes. And you don't think that tells everyone something about you?!!"

On further reflection he may have had a point. Another deal skill.

Free is $10 cheaper than $1

Here's how we presented customized opportunities to receive the *Universal Encyclopedia* (the world's search engine before there *were* search engines).

> **Me:** "Recommendations from real custom-
> ers are our most persuasive selling tool.
> So we're making an *exclusive* offer only
> available to the *first* person in each neigh-
> borhood who gives us their written tes-
> timonial. As soon as we get one we go
> somewhere else."

We dangled *scarcity* and *time pressure*. Key deal tactics.

> **Me:** "I saved the most amazing part for last.
> If you're lucky enough to be the first
> folks chosen, you'll receive a free set of
> encyclopedias and free bookshelves to
> display them on. You heard that right.
> They're *free*."

The purchase price wasn't $100. It wasn't $50. It wasn't $10. The purchase price was *free*!! Accurate and truthful while being simultaneously completely disingenuous and misleading.

Who among us can resist "fabulous" or "free" or "exclusive"? Key deal insights.

Of course, there were some minor details.

The encyclopedia volumes were genuinely free. The accompanying bookcase genuinely was free.

What *wasn't* free was ten years of annual updates the customer had to pay for by check on signing. They knew the purchase price.

Can you guess what the all-in actual cost was? You're a cynical winner if you surmised that by remarkable coincidence the ten-year total payments for the updates equaled the full cost of a set of encyclopedias with matching bookcase.

Whatever today's customer wants to buy is what you're selling today

What follows wasn't part of our training.

I asked every prospective customer to tell me their life story, beginning with their childhood. Most actively enjoyed answering. A handful refused. If they did, I never pressed them. It was a question, not an interrogation.

However most happily answered. People like talking about themselves.

> **Me:** "Where did you grow up?"
>
> "What did you want to be when you grew up?"
>
> "Where did you go to school?"

It seemed much easier to let my customer (and later my counterparties) tell me things they valued and what appealed to them rather than guessing. I learned *how* and (more importantly) *why* they made decisions. Depending on how they curated their life story, I could choose how best to present the encyclopedia story with the maximum probability of a sale.

How you introduce a product, and the context you surround it with, dramatically shapes how someone else perceives it.

> **Customer** (telling life story): "... and after that I dropped out of high school to help support my family. My lack of formal education is the biggest regret of my life."

You'd be well-advised mentioning encyclopedias are the road to college for the customer's children and the key to their brighter future. They just told you how much they valued family and education. That's what this encyclopedia could be to them.

An even more expansive answer on the same theme was,

> **Me:** "These books are more than just an encyclopedia; they're an *entire reference library.*"

Talk about framing big!

Some elements of a presentation had limits. No matter what I learned about a customer and what product I'd like to be selling, the physical dimensions and contents of an encyclopedia set never changed. They were what they were.

That said, listening before presenting helped me explore emotional levers which might motivate this customer to purchase. What vision of an encyclopedia and its benefits did they want to buy? What verbal picture should be painted to best appeal to this customer's self-identified desires and needs?

Listen patiently. Listen quietly. Listen with empathy.

Finding out what this customer or counterparty wants to buy, focusing on their personal value proposition, and then selling that to them is more effective than guessing, whether you're negotiating deals or selling encyclopedias. Persuading someone is fine; deceiving them is not.

What the customer's money should best be used for, what they can or cannot afford, isn't a judgment for you to make. In "St. Stephen" the Grateful Dead cast their own spin on the 18th century observation that "one Man's Loss becomes another Man's Gain."

If a car buyer tells the sales person they want the fastest car on the market, an attentive seller will only talk about speed and horsepower. They won't talk about the car's exterior, sound system, safety devices, trunk size, or color.

It's still the same car, but this customer has emphatically said what they want to buy. You're selling to *them*, not your next customer.

Getting past price

An encyclopedia's cost was not immaterial for our customers, generating legitimate doubts and concerns about affordability and comparative value to them. My untutored reaction was ineffective verging on counterproductive.

I downplayed the issue, shuffled my feet, ignored the question, and continued talking as if the purchase price wasn't problematical.

But it *was*. ***You can only spend the same dollar one time.***

I slowly learned not to deny the obvious validity in a counterparty's statements while also recasting the question and perception of affordability.

Coaching from my encyclopedia mentors improved my approach:

> **Customer:** "That's an awful lot of money to spend on annual updates. Isn't it?"
>
> **Me:** "*Great* question. I respect and appreciate your cost concerns. Thanks for sharing."
>
> "Interesting you raised that. Other folks who received their free encyclopedia and bookshelf said exactly the same thing before signing up."
>
> **Customer:** "That makes me feel better knowing it's a normal question. Why did they sign?"
>
> **Me:** "What changed their mind? They figured out they got this incredible value for only a quarter per day; just two dimes and a nickel. Isn't that amazingly cheap?"

Acknowledge and validate a counterparty's legitimate concerns. Pivot. Reframe. More deal skills.

"A spoonful of sugar helps the medicine go down"

Besides learning how to watch, hear, and employ the magic of framing, I also learned more subtle skills like the value of gentle flattery.

Encyclopedia salesperson (to every customer):	"All of the young intelligent people I've talked with, *just like yourself*, have said the very same thing about the *Universal Encyclopedia* ..."
Buyer to Seller (or **Seller to Buyer**):	"You must have lost twenty pounds. You look sensational; so trim and fit. What's your secret?"

The tricky balance is that these types of engagements are useful and appropriate *only* if they're either obvious flattery received with good humor by the customer, or accurate and delivered with genuine authenticity and sincerity.

Either way how can you not like and trust someone so discerning that they noticed you're young, intelligent, and trim? That's definitely someone *I* trust and want to do business with. A person of rare good judgment. ***Groveling and pandering are underrated virtues.***

Sign the contract. Get the check. Leave the house!

If the decision-making customer said "Yes, we'll buy the encyclopedia" and their spouse did the same (or at least didn't object) that automatically initiated three action steps.

- Get the customer's testimonial and non-negotiable, preprinted, single page, sales contract *signed,*
- get the *check* and (most importantly),
- *leave* the house. *IMMEDIATELY.*

After finalizing a sale by signing the contract, continued interaction with your customer (or counterparty) only fosters an opportunity for second thoughts, for "Buyer's Remorse" to set in. A chance for their "yes" to change into "no."

Customer and spouse (to themselves twenty minutes later):	"Why did we just buy an encyclopedia when we haven't had the money to take a vacation in ten years? What were we thinking? How do we get out of this?"

If you had already left their home, that conversation happens with only *two* people present, wife and husband. Nothing bad happens to you or your sale. You have the signed purchase order, the check, and you're gone.

But if *three* people are still in their home twenty minutes later (and one of them is you) something entirely different occurs.

Customer and spouse (to encyclopedia seller):	"Cancel the order." "Give me back my check." "Leave our house. IMMEDIATELY!"

Something bad did happen to you and your sale. You lost it by lingering.

INDUSTRY TIP: No one buys two sets of encyclopedias.

Why would you stay in a house and keep talking after you closed the sale? You can't sell the same encyclopedia more than once without going to jail for fraud, so you're not going to sell a second one. Staying cannot result in more sales. All risk. No reward.

Claim victory. Stop talking. Leave the house!

Armed with those tactical tidbits, join me in experiencing how encyclopedia selling evolved into this observation.

Selling and negotiating may not be identical twins, but they're no worse than first cousins.

On to our first corporate adventure, some color commentary, and a stark introduction into navigating an unexpected deal world with no playbook or GPS guidance.

SPOILER ALERT. Encyclopedia selling is easier than negotiating business deals. Unlike onetime interactions, deals unfold over weeks and months. "Tactical empathy" (short-lived wiles and crocodile smiles) is exposed. Establishing "Sustainable Deal Empathy" is essential. Genuine bonding builds a level of shared values and beliefs, as well as a form of intimacy. That's the evolved mature approach to strive for.

Chapter 1 Key Takeaways

- In the short run, six primordial emotional factors initially motivate people to decide to buy or sell products or companies;

  1. fear,
  2. greed,
  3. scarcity,
  4. time-pressure,
  5. ego, or
  6. perceived self-interest.

Later they try to justify their choices unemotionally and logically.

- Everyone's decision-making matrix is different. You uncover it through engaged listening, asking open-ended questions, and evaluating responses. That's the only way to knowledgeably frame the optimal customer value proposition for this specific customer.

- Successful salespeople check assumptions at the door. They observe what *is* happening and being said rather than acting based on what they *expected* to occur or hear.

Why guess when you could ask?

- The best appraisal elicits the "5 *W's*," the secret to understanding customers/counterparties.

  - *Who* are the decision-makers,

  - *what* do they want,

  - *when* and *where* do they want to buy it, and

  - *why* do they want to buy it?

That sequence avoids unproductive autopilot and familiarity traps.

- After selling a product (or achieving agreement on a negotiating point), only bad things happen if you keep talking, lingering, or doing anything other than taking these three, straightforward action steps:

  - sign the contract,

  - get the money, and (most importantly)

  - leave the house.

CHAPTER 2

A DEAL MADE IN HEAVEN

Like theater, dealmaking is sometimes possible only by the "willing suspension of disbelief."

We've all watched movies featuring physically impossible actions. Gal Gadot (*Wonder Woman*) isn't really flying unaided through thin air. We know that. Yet for our own reasons we willingly accept an incongruity and embrace the illusion throughout the performance.

We gain by doing so. We want to believe.

The deal world is not always dissimilar.

An experienced buyer's deal team (including me) went to a "get-to-know-you-and-say-hello" meeting with Paul, the CEO-sole owner of Paul's Parts. We had no expectation of anything happening then and there. This was long-term prospecting.

If the CEO were ever going to sell his company in the future, we hoped he'd reach out to us first. All his product lines were complementary (not competitive) to ours. We anticipated a pleasant, unmemorable meeting. We were planting deal seeds, hoping to convey we were financially capable, enthusiastic, and interested. That's all.

It was 10 o'clock on a west coast Tuesday morning. I was there in my dual capacity as a Director (as well as outside lawyer) for a strategic industry buyer (Charley's Consolidated), a well-known public company acquiror.

The CEO's office walls were filled to overflowing with artifacts and paintings affiliated with a particular religious denomination.

After welcoming us he immediately mentioned he was a devout, deeply observant member of his religious congregation. We had no inkling why he shared that unsolicited information but politely acknowledged it. His comments were consistent with what our eyes were seeing.

His next statement was considerably more dramatic and instantly captured our collective attention.

> **CEO-owner:** "I believe your CEO is a Messenger from God."

We were taken aback but didn't correct him. Any reason someone agrees with you is the right reason. If that's what the seller believed, who were we to question his belief?

Don't quarrel with convictions that favor you.

> **Me:** "Interesting, what makes you say that?"

> **CEO-owner:** "Last weekend the world-wide leader of my religious community unexpectedly told me that I'm leaving the country this coming Saturday on a multi-year missionary mission. If you buy my business by this Thursday, I'll know your CEO is a Messenger from God. And if you don't, I'll know he isn't."

Buyer's deal team had decades of extensive personal and professional relationships with our CEO. We were unwavering in our belief that our CEO was *not* a messenger from God.

But maybe we were wrong.

Maybe every circle isn't round.

Maybe our CEO *was* a messenger from God. (He'd almost have to be for us to start a corporate acquisition from scratch on Tuesday and close it on Thursday).

We listened respectfully.

The CEO-owner was extremely smart and mature. His opening statement wasn't impulsive or a negotiating ploy. We took him literally and seriously about the deal timetable and his personal motivation for selling.

As Dealjammers we chose to conduct ourselves within the CEO-owner's story as revealed by him. Success mandated that we negotiate from the reference point presented, so we willingly suspended our disbelief.

Operating within his framework didn't mean we had to agree he was right about our CEO's religious status; nor did we feel compelled to say he was wrong. Regardless of our belief system and perspective, the Seller is entitled to his faith, opinion about our CEO, and point of view regardless of whether that intersects with ours or not.

At a purely pragmatic level, Paul was the Founder, sole owner, and sole decision-maker for the entire enterprise. Deal empathy and deal reality equally dictated we try to see the world through his eyes and respond accordingly.

What negotiating universe were we in, and what were the never-before-contemplated rules?

He told us what he valued. He told us what he wanted. He told us what would motivate him to sell. Those were the rules.

CEO Paul then introduced his deal team. It didn't take long.

The troupe consisted entirely of a bright young solo practitioner who had recently begun a general legal practice. The attorney handled anything and everything, from residential house sales to slip-and-falls at the local Walmart. The lawyer had no experience (legal or otherwise) buying or selling businesses.

What the attorney *did* have was an unshakeable shared faith and belief system with his client. The CEO-owner comfortably relied on his fellow congregant's advice despite the inexperience.

That was problematical through *our* eyes. Having nothing to do with intelligence, people lacking confidence, experience, or knowledge tend to deny counterparty requests or fail to reach sensible compromises. "No" is their default response to suggestions beyond their knowledge or domain expertise (their comfort zone).

Is there anything you've ever done for the first time that was the best you ever did it?

Me neither.

Negotiating complex business or legal issues has the same limitation.

From general information gathered prior to the meeting at trade-shows we knew Seller manufactured several valuable product lines with branded names that interested us. That's why we were there.

What we *didn't* know was that as a legal matter those assets were housed in four separate corporations, each owned entirely by the CEO-owner.

Some deals are difficult; some are implausible. Our mission was now *spectacularly* implausible, officially verging on impossible.

From a standing start our portion of the DealCircle had slightly more than two days to buy four companies. Not as much work as making four separate acquisitions from four different sellers, but mounds more paper, diligence, and risk than acquiring only a single company.

None of the conventional sources of deal data (i.e., Seller's financial statements, operational analysis, customer list, or personnel detail) had been exchanged or reviewed prior to our informal meeting. No due diligence. No purchase price negotiation.

A comparable acquisition moving at conventional speed would routinely involve (more or less) three months of document re-view, coupled with drafting and negotiating upward of 15 major and ancillary agreements. Maybe slightly less than two months if all DealCirclers were phenomenally motivated, competent, and available.

Could you make it any harder? (To be clear, that's the first of countless rhetorical questions.)

Nonetheless we were highly motivated and undaunted.

Seller's operations and product lines were crown jewels that would easily integrate into Buyer's sales and distribution channel. Seller's operations included numerous branded products, quality engineers, management, as well as loyal customers.

Like most strategic buyers, our analysis was we'd make more money by owning Paul's Parts operations than Paul could. We could cut costs, eliminate duplicate corporate overhead, and buy raw materials in bulk, as well as increasing revenues by selling *our* products to *his* customers while selling *his* products to *our* existing customer base.

Scarcity sells. Scarcity motivates.

There were no comparable "targets" for Buyer to acquire. The CEO-owner had built a fabulous, one-of-a-kind, manufacturing business from nothing. Extremely hard for us to duplicate by ourselves or acquire elsewhere.

Seller was in an unusual, highly desirable position. He didn't have to do a deal with us or anyone. He was equally happy to sell or not sell. The four businesses were so well run that if CEO-owner left his team in charge and went away for two years, operations would run as smoothly as the justifiably time-honored Swiss watch.

All the pressure was on *us*. All the leverage was *his*.

Knowing he believed we were there on behalf of a Messenger from God, we were relieved when he didn't request a miracle purchase price.

His "ask" was well-within industry-standard parameters. Comparable businesses were selling for 6-8 times their previous twelve months' cashflow. He asked for nine times; hardly a show-stopper.

As an experienced acquirer our typical pattern would have been weeks of offers, counter-offers, and counter-counter-offers to aggressively accomplish three goals:

- reduce purchase *price,*
- improve purchase *terms,* and
- *structure* the transaction to maximally protect us as Buyer.

Regrettably that wasn't a choice.

Time is the invisible but palpable enemy.

That maxim is (almost) always true in the deal world but rarely so nakedly obvious. We were keenly aware of the fragile critical path to Closing. With the deal clock ticking, even small delays would cause us to fail to meet the deadline. *Every negotiator needs a metronome.*

Before lunchtime we settled on a token purchase price decrease.

Two *hours* instead of two *weeks* to reach price agreement. Unheard of, but *Necessity is the Mother of Everything.*

More problematical than price were Seller's proposed deal *structure* and *terms.*

Why?

BRIEF LEGAL DETOUR BEGINS

To avoid bogging down in technical minutiae, certain legal, tax, and accounting concepts will be over-simplified and treated only at a high level. Sometimes the collective factors favor *stock* purchases and other times *asset* purchases. It depends, and it's usually a less-than-perfect tradeoff.

Frequently a buyer's primary structural consideration is avoiding becoming responsible for a seller's liabilities (particularly unknown or contingent). That's a much easier decision.

Buyers purchase only specific *assets* (and assume only specific *liabilities*) from the selling *company.* They don't buy stock from the company's *stockholders.* (The *who* makes an enormous difference.)

It's easier to get money back from someone if you never gave it to them.

Buyers know less about Seller's business than Seller. To bridge this information asymmetry, Seller makes contractual, factual representations (reps) for Buyer to rely on, such as:

- My historical financial statements are accurate.
- Accounts receivable on my balance sheet are collectible.
- No one's suing me.

What if those aren't true? That would be a misrepresentation.

Other than commercial rep and warranty insurance (not always available or affordable), Buyer's easiest legal and practical protection against Seller's misrepresentations is self-help. Buyer pays only part of the purchase price to Seller at Closing ("Closing Cash"), with the balance paid later ("Deferred Cash").

Common methods to pay the post-Closing portion of a purchase price?

- *Escrow*. Place Deferred Cash into a segregated account with an independent party (like a bank) for a fixed period of time as a source of cash to pay Buyer's valid claims for Seller's misrepresentations (if any),

- *Promissory Note*. Pay Deferred Cash with a promissory note from Buyer to Seller payable in the future ("DealDebt"), or

- *Contingent payments*. In addition to Closing Cash, more cash price is payable (if and only if) agreed-to business performance targets are achieved by Buyer with Seller's business.

If Buyer has a post-Closing claim against Seller, all three methods provide Buyer some control over unpaid purchase price. With legal justification Buyer can refuse paying DealDebt (or releasing money from escrow) and keep money equaling the claimed amount.

To my relief and yours, our ...

BRIEF LEGAL DETOUR ENDS

Seller wanted us to:

- buy *stock* of four separate companies,
- from their sole stockholder,
- who was immediately leaving the country, *and*
- pay the entire purchase price in cash at Closing.

If Seller-CEO defrauded us, we'd have a hard time *finding* him let alone *suing* him to get our money back—the structural equivalent of the Four Horsemen of the Apocalypse. In my Dad's colorful phrasing, we'd be financially exposed and "naked as a grape."

After fruitless negotiations (and considerable agita within Buyer's deal team) we relied on Seller's industry-wide reputation for integrity, took a major-league leap of faith, agreed to buy stock (not assets), and pay the full purchase price at Closing. With most sellers, we'd have quickly walked away from the deal.

(For the curious among you, all four companies turned out to be squeaky clean, highly profitable, and folded easily into our sales channel.)

In a now-unimaginable world before ubiquitous personal computers we started creating lengthy documents from the ground up: an ugly, time-consuming process.

We agreed with Seller on a basic form of Acquisition and Non-Competition Agreement. Then we conformed that document to each corporation's slightly different facts and financial statements.

Piles of people and paper to process.

A long day's journey into two M&A nights

Our entire team worked straight through (without sleeping) from Tuesday morning until Closing late on Thursday afternoon. (It probably helped that although Buyer's team were deal veterans, no one was much older than Seller's attorney.)

At 3:00 a.m. (on Wednesday night/Thursday morning) we finished negotiating all purchase agreements. Then we started negotiating an "Employment and Noncompetition Agreement" with Seller's extremely talented Senior Vice President (SVP), Amara.

Notwithstanding her vague title, she effectively functioned as Seller's Chief Operating Officer (COO) as well as Chief Financial Officer (CFO). She ran day-to-day operations and finance with finesse and competence. Reaching agreement with her was critical to a smooth ownership transition and ongoing business success.

We had no operating personnel who could take over for her, didn't have enough time to recruit a successor, and had no desire to do so.

Our need was extreme. The CEO-owner would be gone and unavailable to provide transition assistance and stability after Closing. She *was* the institutional corporate memory, anchoring go-forward relationships with customers and employees.

Said differently, Amara's negotiating leverage was short of astronomical but nonetheless substantial. Not meaningfully less than Paul's. We addressed our compensation proposal simultaneously to her as well as counsel. Before we finished the young lawyer interrupted:

Young Lawyer: "I can't represent her because I'm representing the company as well as CEO-owner. That would be a conflict of interest."

Me: "I admire your strong sense of legal ethics. You're probably technically right. Even so our mutual problem is there are fewer than twelve hours to meet your client's deadline. Are you thinking it's likely she'll find another lawyer at three o'clock in the morning?"

Young Lawyer: "Doesn't matter. I *can't* represent her."

A long, uncomfortable, very tired silence ensued. Not obvious to any of us how to proceed. Then the DealCircle's collective discomfort was broken in an unlooked-for manner.

CEO-owner:	*"I'll* represent my Senior Vice President."
***Everyone* on the buy side:**	"Say what? Now we're completely confused. If *anyone* has a conflict it's *you*. We're paying you $10 million, and you won't get it unless we have a deal with her. Oh, and I'm just sayin', you're not a lawyer."
Senior Vice President:	"I have complete trust in my CEO to represent me. We're in the same congregation."
Me:	"O-h-h-h-h-h-kay. Well if Amara isn't represented by a lawyer, legal ethics mean *I* can't represent Buyer. Our outside accountant will represent *us*."

Consider the logic (or illogic) of this. The non-lawyer CEO-owner "represented" his own Senior VP to avoid a conflict. It's worth repeating that her employment agreement was the solitary obstacle between him and $10 million.

The less flexible among us (or merely less tired) might easily see the CEO's situation as the definition of an unwaivable conflict preventing him from even being involved in the discussion.

But every day (and some nights) offers a fresh opportunity to learn and evolve.

I stepped aside as Buyer's counsel. Our CPA negotiated on our behalf.

To my relief, both "advocates" negotiated vigorously and did a fine job of representing their respective "clients." From all appearances, they relished demonstrating they were smarter than their lawyers.

Of course, that's a fairly low bar to exceed. (Pun intended, even if not welcomed).

It's still not clear to me how this solved either the conflict of interest or competent legal representation problem. But some ideas are acceptable at three in the morning that wouldn't be during standard business hours. Once again, we rolled with an alternative reality.

Adrenaline was running low as exhaustion was rising. We were nearing the limits of our emotional ability to "go with the flow" and willingly suspend disbelief.

Which made yet one more *Alice in Wonderland* moment untimely and unwelcome.

After our Brief Legal Detour, we know Buyers purchasing stock justifiably rely on seller's contractual "representations." If they're inaccurate (i.e., Seller misrepresented a fact about the business) Seller owes Buyer money equaling the financial damage.

These are Seller's minimum factual representations:

- The Company you're purchasing exists.
- Seller owns the stock you're buying.
- After Closing you'll own the entire Company you paid for.

Those seem reasonable, don't they?

Lawyers for sellers deliver formal "opinion letters" confirming those representations from a legal perspective, peppered with some weaselly, lawyer-like disclaimers. Not this Seller's attorney.

Young Lawyer: "I can't give a legal opinion about any of those things.

"I wasn't present when the Company was formed.

"I wasn't there when Seller bought the stock.

"I personally don't know if the Company exists, or the CEO-owner paid for the stock, or if the stock was validly issued.

"All I know for sure is his name is listed in all four corporate record books next to Stock Certificate No. 1."

We suspended our suspension.

Third-party realities left us zero flexibility. In Jerry Garcia's words,

> *... we are not completely autonomous. At some point or another, our boundaries run into the boundaries of the exterior reality...and other things...we don't have control over.*

Without Seller's representations and corresponding legal opinion our bank wouldn't let us borrow the money for the $10 million purchase price. Without money we couldn't close. Not complicated.

One of my maxims kicked in. ***No one is more unreasonable than a reasonable person whose patience has been exhausted.***

Me: "This really isn't the time or place for a philosophical debate about whether the company exists or not.

"After 48 hours of negotiating I don't even know if *you* exist or *I* exist. But for purposes of this conversation I'm willing to assume *you* exist, and you'll have to assume *I* exist.

"If we get your legal opinion and your client's representations, we'll transfer $10 million to Paul's account in about nine hours.

"If you don't, or he doesn't, we can't, so we won't.

"No wiggle room. No compromises. No appeasement. We're not willing or able to go down this rabbit hole with you."

After CEO and Young Lawyer huddled privately for about twenty minutes, the following down-to-earth responses occurred.

CEO-owner: "I'll make the representations."

Young Lawyer: "I'll give the matching opinion of counsel."

It struck me that while CEO-owner may have been pious, beatification may not have been in his immediate future.

With that settled I phoned our banker to let her know for the first time we were borrowing $10 million under our existing loan, usually a multi-day process.

I reached Yanwei at her home before breakfast on Thursday morning. Somewhat grumpily and groggily she said:

> **Banker:** "Marc, do you know what time it is?"

> **Me:** "Yes I do. It's three o'clock on *Thursday* morning where I am. I've been awake since *Tuesday* morning at seven o'clock local time. I definitely know what time it is. But it's only six o'clock Thursday morning where you are. Isn't that right?"

My question was predictably rhetorical, so I didn't wait for a reply.

> **Me:** "We need $10 million placed in Buyer's corporate account immediately. Less than six hours from now you'll deposit that money to the account of a seller you know nothing about, to fund a deal you know nothing about. I don't see any problems, do you?"

Armed with that explanation (and no doubt aided by my "cheery" voice) Yanwei "de-grumped." Money was deposited and (at our request) sent to Seller a few hours later. We closed a few hours after that.

Years later it occurred to me what a dramatic, theatrical presentation the CEO-owner had unintentionally "staged." What incredible framing for this negotiation and sale.

His office displays of religious artifacts and paintings weren't altered for the purpose of meeting with or impressing us. In that physical context Paul's opening comments about our CEO being a Messenger from God made perfect sense.

If Seller-CEO had used the same language (and made the same assertion) on a phone or Zoom-type call he wouldn't have convinced any of us. The sentence and sentiment would have seemed artificial or contrived. Our skepticism meter would have registered off the charts.

But his office *was* who he was. His analysis of our CEO was his normal. We called him; he didn't call us. Nothing was staged. His walls powerfully and persuasively reinforced the meaning and conviction of his words.

This was organic deal theater, stagecraft, and framing at their finest. No encyclopedia seller could have done better.

And so, onward and upward to the next adventure on a lighter note.

Making a sale's splash with soup

In most business situations it's helpful (and sometimes legally imperative) to "know your customer." Except when it isn't. Every now and again it's *unhelpful* to be overly conscious of your counterparty's background and culture.

A Berlin-based company was buying expensive (tens of millions of dollars), large-scale construction equipment from a Detroit-headquartered business. My law firm represented Buyer whenever they did business in the United States. The Detroit construction company's CEO (let's call him Joey) was eager to sell some equipment (not the company) and invited my clients and me to a relatively informal lunch at his country club.

Unlike Paul's potent natural staging, Joey's was somewhat contrived. Not genuine like Paul's office (and so less powerful), but not a bad idea. Usually, it's helpful to have some personal relationship-building visiting time before getting to technical specifications and price negotiations.

Alas, the best laid plans of mice, women, and men often go awry. As soon as we were seated Joey began his well-intentioned conversational icebreaker:

> **CEO:** "You should really try the cold tomato and cucumber soup they make here. Our club serves the best Gestapo soup I've ever had."

> **Everyone else** (stunned): "Wait. Did he really just say '*Gestapo* soup'?"

All assembled struggled with how to respond.

Buyer's all-German personnel were visibly angry and confused. Had they just been insulted intentionally or unintentionally?

Did Joey really mean to say *gazpacho* soup but mispronounced it? Were Buyers being overly sensitive about their country's role in World War II so they projected those concerns and misheard what he said?

Seller's DealCircle (other than the mortified CEO) desperately tried to stifle laughter while simultaneously trying to figure out how to pretend none of us heard what we just heard.

Awkward. Very, *very* awkward.

To say the least, Gestapo soup is a memorable phrase leaving an indelible negative impression. Do you think that's what Joey would have said if Buyer's personnel were from Idaho? Or Ireland? Or India?

Me neither.

Fortunately profit and necessity are powerful commercial motivators.

- Despite what Joey *said*, his company made the best machine in the world.
- Despite what we all *heard*, Buyer needed the best machine.

- Despite an all-time great Freudian slip, the sale closed and Buyer ordered several machines.

I remain skeptical as to whether Seller or Buyer added each other to their respective holiday card lists.

On to the next corporate caper.

Chapter 2 Key Takeaways

- *Negotiating is Theater with consequences and results.* Staging and framing aren't necessarily in conflict with honest dealings.

Done well, they're powerful persuaders. Done poorly (patently artificial or reeking of insincerity), your credibility will be undermined before the negotiation starts.

- *Any* reason your counterparty agrees with you is the *right* reason. **Don't quarrel with convictions that favor you.**

Their perspective on life will rarely mirror yours. You're trying to do a specific deal with this specific counterparty. The better you understand *them* and what *they* value, the more effective you'll be at identifying and addressing their *real* needs and not their wish list of *stated* needs.

Talk less. Listen more. Remain open to possibility.

- Embrace genuine deadlines. If they don't exist, create them.

Believable deadlines give all DealCirclers permission to let little stuff go. If they don't, the deal will run out of time and energy before the deal runs out of issues.

Focus only on major issues. If those are resolved, everything else falls into place. If they're not, there *is* no deal, so you're not losing an actual opportunity.

- Deal *flexibility* is good but can't be infinite. Distinguish "*nice*-to-haves" from "*need*-to-haves." If you get the "needs-to-haves," you're better off doing the deal than if you don't. And vice versa.

"A ROSE BY ANY OTHER NAME MAY SMELL AS SWEET" BUT MOST BUYERS WON'T PAY AS MUCH FOR IT

In the corporate middle market, you routinely encounter owners who are first-time business sellers.

They're corporate finance rookies who never sold a business before, and likely will never sell a business again. Deep emotional involvement combined with inexperience creates unexpected vulnerabilities.

Think about NFL rookie quarterbacks. Sportscasters usually note their first-year status, predict they'll throw interceptions, and expect them to have trouble reading defenses.

Those mistakes and vulnerabilities don't come from a lack of talent or intelligence. We all draw statistically invalid conclusions from statistically invalid data samples. Rookies in any arena (football or corporate) lack sufficient on-the-field/in-the-game data to have formed real-time pattern recognition. That only comes with experience.

Deal fragility increases if the business was founded by Seller (or their family) and includes second generation (and later) relatives as stakeholders. Overcompensated (and underperforming) family member employees might be shocking but should never surprise.

All deals are personal, but Founders are more so

Founders are different from non-Founders in some incredibly positive ways. These are individuals who create something from nothing through immense willpower and a self-confidence bordering on arrogance. To succeed they routinely live at the boundary of the "hallucinogenically" optimistic.

A Founder's self-identity, executive position and title, business ownership, and net worth are inextricably intertwined. The company represents a lifetime of love and labor. It's literally their name on the corporate door; it's their child.

Negotiations to sell their business reflect that complex passion and are intensely personal and emotionally charged. Every dollar of purchase price paid (or not paid) flows to the owner, an audience of one.

With no supporting analysis, many want (and feel entitled to) what in polite society is referred to as "walk-away money." Everyone's idea of what constitutes walk-away money varies. The numbers are different. Not better. Not worse. No judgment.

Hugely different than more dispassionate and analytical interactions between public company executives involving the same business. Deal dollars coming (or going) between Company A and Company B would *not* flow directly to either negotiator's individual wallet.

The contrast?

> **Founder:**   "It's *my* bank account we're talking about. Not corporate treasury's balance sheet."

Relinquishing ownership, control, and role by selling their business impacts the Founder's total existence. No matter how much money they receive, experiencing loss is still part of their new reality. Their entire life mosaic has to be rearranged.

It's like your iPhone but on steroids.

If you jiggle an app on your home screen and move it elsewhere, all your other apps move to fill the vacant space. The result is an unfamiliar reconfiguration of your home screen that may confuse you even though all the apps are still there.

Now try to imagine if your home screen were your life screen. Without their business Founders have a huge void in the rhythm of their life with nothing obvious to fill it except a pile of cash.

Selling their business triggers unanswerable human, non-economic questions.

> **Prospective Seller** (talking to themselves): "The price is more-than-acceptable, but if I sell my company what will I do every day? Where will I go? How will I introduce myself when meeting new people? Will I still be relevant? Will I start saying 'I used to be somebody'?"

Success selling encyclopedias hinged on recognizing that verbal abuse and objections you encountered weren't personal. They were noise, not signal.

The opposite applies as dealmakers encounter Founders (and their families). Founder counterparties will hear everything you say about the company *personally* no matter how politely you frame it or how impersonally you mean it. Their responses keenly reflect that.

Statements of unpleasant facts about the quality of Seller's corporate earnings are experienced as direct attacks on Founder as individuals. Seller won't ignore them.

(In your daily life, you've probably noticed telling proud parents their baby is ugly isn't a good way to win friends or influence people.)

The more accurate your observation about a negative aspect of the business (the Founder's metaphorical baby), the more likely you are to produce outraged anger and defensiveness.

Get back to me on whether you think the following is a good way to approach Seller's bloated balance sheet:

> **Buyer** (after reviewing Seller's financial statements): "Gee, having 120 days outstanding of customer receivables (instead of a well-run company's 45-60 days) must be killing your cash flow. I'm involved in lots of companies and this is the worst cash management I've ever seen."

Still, a fact is a fact, no matter how well (or ill) received.

If payment is allowed four months after goods have been shipped or services performed, the financially weakest, most marginal customers buy from Seller. No competitor sells on such lax payment terms.

Customers are receiving the equivalent of an unsecured loan. At best, Seller receives the full amount the customer owes but without interest. All other alternatives are worse.

With this financial approach, Sellers:

- won't collect numerous receivables,
- will experience unusually high default rates from customers, and
- under-reserve doubtful accounts on Seller's balance sheet.

Here's an illustration:

Seller's balance sheet reflects $100 of customer receivables with a $5 "reserve" against that. In financial-speak Seller is saying they'll collect $95 of cash (i.e., $100 of balance sheet receivables minus $5 reserve for bad debts).

Realistically they're more likely to collect $90.

As receivables get older (number of days outstanding from date of invoice increases) they get progressively more uncollectible. (Most formula-based bank loan agreements won't include receivables greater than 90 days old in calculating how much a borrower can borrow.) That's a problem.

The result?

Seller's income was overstated by $5 on its financial statements. Seller's net worth was overstated by the same amount. The toxic dilemma?

If Buyer doesn't call out those factors as material negatives to the business's true value, rest assured Seller will not.

You can't even be absolutely certain that Seller *recognizes* the problem or adverse financial valuation consequences of its credit and payment policies; they may simply be bad managers.

In a perfect world Buyer coaxes *Seller* into acknowledging bad facts about Seller's business, avoiding unnecessary emotional confrontations. Let the baby be identified as ugly from Seller's mouth, not yours.

Buyer (with innocent tones): "Thanks for sharing your financial statements with me. I'm probably reading them wrong. Like the rest of the industry, our customers pay us 30 days after we bill them. It almost looks like you only collect cash from your customers three months later (120 days after invoice date).

"That can't be right, can it? Wouldn't that create an incredible cash flow problem? You're a great manager so that's not possible."

What's Seller supposed to do? Deny they're a great manager?

Seller: "We have lots of cash. We're just very customer friendly. We don't hound customers to pay in 30 days. That's a major reason why we have such loyal customers. A sale is a sale. Stop nitpicking."

Buyer (with butter not melting from their mouth): "That's really commendable and to your credit as a kind human being. The more sales you make, the less cash you have to run your business. It's like continuously lending money to your customers without charging them for it; sort of a negative cash flow machine."

The more Seller sells the "behinder" Seller gets.

Buyer: "Do you compensate for that cash drain by paying your suppliers, employees, and landlord every 120 days? That would even it out. If we buy your company, we'd expect customer payments within 30 days. We'd lose some of your customers and sales. Revenues and profit would shrink.

If we took your approach, our borrowing from our bank would go up. Unlike you, they charge interest. Our lender would make more money, but we wouldn't."

Whose baby is ugly?

The Founder's baby is ugly. *Very* ugly.

But while raising significant issues about Seller's dangerous use of capital and less-than-solid revenues, we've called the Founder "smart, generous, and kind." What could they disagree with?

Buyer's logic chain leaves Seller with two unattractive choices. Seller can:

- correct Buyer and argue they were "stupid, selfish, or mean," or alternatively,

- agree their corporate baby was undeniably ugly.

Most Sellers would rather acknowledge a flawed business model than agree that they're stupid. So they will.

Issues that typically wouldn't arise with a corporate owner (or even a non-founder) are commonly issues with Founders, expressed with unexpected vehemence. Emotion shreds logic; distorting judgment and memory.

With total sincerity a Founder looks at you and says,

> **Founder:** "All those museum-quality paintings, antiques, and Persian rugs in my corporate office, plus the car I drive, belong to *me*. I paid for them personally. They're not part of the business you're buying because the company doesn't own them."

> **Buyer:** "That's confusing. All of them are specifically listed on your company's balance sheet and have been depreciated as corporate assets."

> **Founder:** "Well, the accountants made a mistake."

> **Buyer** (with incredulity): "Every year for *fifteen* years?"

Buyer is right. The company paid for and owns everything in Seller's office.

There's a remote possibility the CEO believes those items were paid for personally. Those objects have been in their office for decades.

Possession is 9/10 of any memory.

Confront or engage? How best to proceed?

INDUSTRY TIP: Calling Seller a liar is *not* recommended.

There's absolutely no doubt this matter is of epic, personal importance to Seller. That creates negotiating opportunity for Buyer. Certain corporate assets or liabilities have "symmetrical *financial* value." The negotiation amounts to a zero-sum game from which either buyer or seller emerges victorious. If one counterparty gains a value, the other loses an equivalent value.

What creates opportunity is that Founder's office possessions represent an "asymmetrical negotiating variable."

The value to Seller is high while the value to Buyer is low. The value to Seller is *emotional* while the value to Buyer is wholly *unemotional* and purely financial.

This isn't the right time to plant your flag in the sand and confront. You're technically correct about corporate ownership of those possessions, but acting on that knowledge right now may not be the smartest thing to do.

Kicking the can down the road is a neutral strategy. It doesn't risk killing deal momentum with an immediate confrontation.

> **Buyer** (kicking the can): "Well, there's obviously some ambiguity on this issue. Our accountants should hash this out with your accountants. They're both competent and fair. Let's see what we learn from them."
>
> or,
>
> **Buyer** (at the other extreme, from a more aggressive posture): "I have to be blunt. This throws me for somewhat of a loop. Part of how we justified offering such a high purchase price was by attributing meaningful value to those paintings, rugs, and car. Really not sure how to proceed."

Meanwhile, returning to Planet Earth, the highest probability is that Buyer attached *no* financial value to those items. Paintings, carpets, and cars aren't operating assets used to generate Seller's corporate revenues and profits.

Truth be told, you weren't even aware they existed until your accountant found them buried in a footnote to Seller's financial statement.

Tuck this impasse away. Chalk it up as a "win-in-waiting."

You know Seller values these assets highly. Surrender them (or trade them for something you genuinely care about) much later in the negotiation as if not acquiring them involves an agonizing and costly concession.

Buyer (much later in the negotiations):	"As I understand it, there are only two unresolved issues. You want to keep the car, rugs, and paintings we were buying?"
Seller:	"Yes."
Buyer:	"We want your noncompetition agreement to be five years not three years."
Seller:	"Yes. That's my understanding."
Buyer:	"Tell you what. We'll give you *all* those possessions (rugs, paintings, and car), if we get five years on the noncompete. Nothing could be fairer. Do we have a deal?"
Seller (relieved):	"Yes."

Buyer set up a nice negotiating rhythm by asking the first two questions. Seller had no choice other than to answer each with a "yes." Answering "yes" the third time simply continued the verbal pattern set by Buyer.

On to a Founder's folly.

Lions and "Tigers" and Bears, oh my!

There were several partners in our investor group formed specifically to acquire Tiger Tights, a family-owned business in the Pacific Northwest. We were all experienced operators and dealmakers, but none had managed this kind of product.

Unlike the strategic acquiror who bought four companies from Paul's Parts, our group had no existing operations to fold Tiger into. By necessity Tiger would operate as a standalone business.

We surfaced as a possible buyer when Tiger's CEO "casually" mentioned to our lead investor that he was eager to shed management burdens as retirement age neared.

Lead investor (to the rest of us):	"I have a friend who is CEO of a relatively sleepy 'lifestyle' company. Nicely profitable. Generates cash even after paying himself an unjustifiably high salary. Stellar consumer reputation for high quality tights and related fashion items. They've never expanded sales beyond their neighboring states. I'd like to buy the business and run it nationally."
Rest of us:	"If you run Tiger you'll quickly:

- *add* a sophisticated sales and distribution channel,

- *reduce* management compensation to market levels, and

- dramatically *increase* customers, revenues, profit, and cash flow.

"What's not to like? We're all in."

From initial contact through protracted negotiations (and almost daily exchange of documents with Tiger's CEO and legal team), every indication was that CEO was the owner, and sole decision-maker on the sell side.

Equity raised. Bank financing arranged. Business plan ready. Team-Buyer poised to execute.

Then a "super-small" unanticipated problem arose.

Every document identified Tiger's sole stockholder as "Tiger Family Trust #1." Wealthy families routinely own major assets this way for estate planning purposes, so the ownership structure by itself raised no red flags.

What wasn't identified was the *Trustee* of the Trust (i.e., the person with legal authority to make decisions and execute Closing documents for them).

Why weren't we alarmed?

We were buying Tiger Tights' stock from its legal owner, the *Trust*. That's who we paid cash to (not the Trustee). As Seller, the Trust was making representations and indemnifying us. For our purposes, the only relevance of the Trustee was that they signed the contracts on behalf of the Trust.

Imagine our shock when Seller's lawyers informed us (the day before Closing) that the CEO *wasn't* the controlling person of Tiger Tights, his wife Madison was. Her Family's last name was "Tiger."

Madison's Mom founded Tiger. At her death the business passed to Madison. She was the Trust's sole Trustee as well as beneficiary.

Out of the blue it was crystal clear who the DealCircle's one-and-only real stakeholder and decision-maker was, Madison (the Reluctant Spouse).

Seller's lawyers told us that after sleepless nights (as the Closing approached and reality of the transaction set in) Madison concluded she would rather not sell her business at all than sell the Tiger name. Non-Family shouldn't be selling products with *her* name on them.

In the moment we didn't know if this was a classic case of:

- "Seller's Remorse,"
- a last-minute attempt to increase purchase price,
- both, or
- something else.

Unintentionally we had violated the cardinal rule of trying to close an encyclopedia sale after only talking with one spouse. Shame on us.

This was our semi-informed conjecture. Tiger Tights had been the small town's largest business and employer throughout Madison's lifetime. She and her husband-CEO were civic VIPs; big fish in a microscopic pond.

What would happen to their community standing if the Tiger Family no longer:

- owned and operated the business,
- paid conspicuously large municipal taxes, and
- provided livelihood to a considerable number of citizens?

Can we all agree it probably wouldn't go up?

The question and conclusion was intensely personal and emotionally devastating. The deal was *off*.

We accepted Seller's lawyer's assurance that the genuine impediment was our ongoing use of the Tiger name. To buy the business, we'd have to change the product name as well as corporate name.

Our Investor Group indulged in ten minutes of self-pity about the unfairness of life, but moved past that rapidly...

OK. OK. That's not what happened. The five of us spent several hours angrily venting our frustration to each other.

"Unbelievable. Shocks the conscience."

"We've been *had* and I am *mad*."

Eventually we pulled ourselves together (pretending to be grownups). Venting wasn't getting us closer to buying the business.

The Tiger brand may not have the global value and name recognition of Ferrari or Apple, but it was seriously good and valuable. Tiger's reputation for quality and fashion leadership was integral to why consumers bought their tights.

There was nothing we could do about the economics of municipal taxes or status as an employer. So we concentrated on overcoming Madison's identified emotional resistance.

Could Buyer use the Tiger name for our corporate purposes while still maintaining the Tiger family's prominence, civic status, and (most importantly) sense of Family pride and comfort level with our business activities.

Tactically we sought to provide ongoing high community visibility for them after an ownership change, proudly display the Tiger Family name, and deeply and permanently connect the Family's generational generosity to the town and its residents.

> **Investor Group:** "Here's our suggestion. We'd be *delighted* to establish a scholarship at the local college endowed with your family name, i.e., the 'Tiger Family Scholarship.' Madison can select the annual recipients and personally award the funds. The Tiger Family will receive public adulation and local media coverage as major civic benefactors."

Our premise was that Madison would speak for the Family and receive direct emotional satisfaction by making the scholarship selection and presentation. Her picture would be taken with the recipient. Her choice would be selected and presented. She would feel as if she had some visibility and control over the future use of the Tiger name.

There was absolutely *no* interest.

Undaunted we varied our approach.

> **Investor Group:** "We have a *spectacular* alternative you'll like even more than the scholarship."

We moved up from our previous self-characterization as "delighted"; intensifying our adjective to *spectacular*, plus adding three new choices.

> **Investor Group:** "We'd be *thrilled* to record the Tiger Family's remarkable personal and corporate history and contributions to the town.
>
> "We'd be *honored* if you'd let us engrave this important narrative in stone and prominently place it at corporate headquarter's entrance.

> "We'd be *privileged* to pay for a privately
> published Family biography. You can give
> all the books you want to whomever you
> want. We'll also display them in our lobby."

Our hope was that *daily* visibility of a stone engraving to every
passerby in town would appeal more than only *annual* adulation
from scholarship giving. Generations of the Tiger Family could
walk by global headquarters and swell with pride.

A book glorifying their activities seemed even more versatile and
tangible than a scholarship. Not location-bound or time-bound.
Something they could give away endlessly, reminding residents and nonresidents alike of the Tiger Family's contributions
to the town.

We Dealjammed, floating never-ending variations on these
themes.

Each modification was centered on spending our money and using
our corporate platform at *our* expense, not hers. No one outside
the DealCircle would ever know we were paying for scholarships,
books, or memorials.

The economic impact of each alternative would increase the
agreed purchase price, but not beyond what we were willing to
pay to salvage the deal.

The credit would be *hers*. The cost would be *ours*.

We twisted. (Think Chubby Checkers.) We improvised. (Think
Grateful Dead.) We Dealjammed.

It was increasingly clear that no affordable economic adjustment
(and probably no economic adjustment at all) was going to eliminate her emotional impediments to Closing.

What we couldn't do as a practical matter was:

- buy the business, and
- delete "Tiger" from the corporate and product name.

So our final offer truly was our final offer.

Investor Group: "We'll give you the perpetual, *free* and *exclusive* right to use the name 'Tiger' for other organizations you control so long as the entity doesn't compete with us.

"Tiger *Charitable Foundation* would be no problem. Tiger Tights isn't a charity.

"Tiger *Tanks* would be *no* problem. No one could confuse tanks with tights.

"Tiger *Toys* would be *no* problem. No one could confuse toys with tights.

"Tiger *Stockings and Shoes,* on the other hand, *would* be a problem."

There was absolutely no interest.

Consumers weren't going to buy Tiger tights from us unless they were labeled "Tiger Tights."

She *wouldn't* give. We *couldn't* give. We *didn't* buy the business.

It's hard to know whether our Investor Group or Tiger's CEO was more frustrated by not closing. *We* lost an exciting investment opportunity. *He* had to go back to work.

As many (including Bob Weir) have noted, "sometimes the magic works, and sometimes the magic doesn't." Sometimes musical or deal jams work, and sometimes they don't. Getting a deal done at any price and on any terms but not getting what you're paying for *isn't* Dealjamming. The technical term for this is "dumb."

Take a bow, get off the stage, and move to the next gig.

Could our thorns have been someone else's roses?

Tiger Tights was the number one branded name in its product category and had been for forty years. Consumers associated it with quality, durability, and fashion.

As a standalone investor buyer, the Tiger name was a material asset to us, arguably *the* material asset. Without that branded name all we had to sell consumers was a low margin, commodity-type product. The company itself would be worth tremendously less than the agreed purchase price.

What if instead of our Investor Group the hopeful Tiger Tights' buyer was a company with $10 billion of annual revenues, abundant established brands, and strong, fashion-related brand and tradenames? We'll call our hypothetical buyer "Florence's Fashions."

Could Florence successfully respond to the last-minute withdrawal of the Tiger Tights' name when we couldn't?

Industry buyer Florence's CEO:	"Finding this out so close to Closing is a real shock. The deal has always included the valuable Tiger branded name. That drives your sales, attracts your customers, and *is* your competitive advantage. It's also *the* economic foundation for our $18 million offer.
	"Without the Tiger name, revenues and profit will plummet. What you want to sell us is a mere fraction of the business our Board approved. Our offer is terminated."
Seller's CEO (very reluctantly):	"I can't disagree."

What did Buyer convey (in fewer than 100 words and less than a minute) about the desirability and financial value of Tiger Tights without the Tiger name, as well as the deal itself?

Buyer's Board of Directors (every counterparty's incalculably valuable "bear in the cage") has just *left* their cage and is now intimately involved and visible in the transaction. Good cop-CEO; bad cop-Directors. That's never a positive for any Seller.

From a purely *economic* perspective, Buyer:

- agreed with Seller about the Family name's value,
- communicated that Tiger Tights' business deteriorates without the Tiger name, and
- explained why sales and profits would decrease post-acquisition, making the business worth less to Buyer today.

From a purely *personal* perspective,

- $18 million in cash wouldn't be delivered to Tiger Family this week, and
- Seller-CEO's retirement has been revoked.

BIG losses.

That brief conversation (seemingly ending this negotiation) nicely sets up Florence's *next* negotiating step, the *follow-up* negotiation.

Unlike us, Florence could re-brand the product to consumers using one of their existing, well-known product names. Maybe "Sally's Stockings?" Florence wouldn't lose a beat or a sale.

After letting negative implications and sense of loss sink in (hours for some and weeks for others), Buyer's CEO would call Seller's CEO to have this much more pointed conversation.

Industry buyer Florence's CEO: "I got really beaten up by my Directors when this deal collapsed. They're not happy with *me*. They're even less happy with *you*."

Seller's CEO: "I understand."

Industry buyer Florence's CEO: "They reluctantly agree you *can* keep the Tiger corporate name. Florence won't identify any products we sell as Tiger. The Board is prepared to close using the already-prepared-documents, with only a single change."

Seller's CEO: "Whatever it is, I'm sure it won't be a problem."

Industry Buyer	"Everywhere the documents currently use
Florence's CEO:	the phrase '$18 million' as the purchase price, that will be changed to '$12 million.' You can't sell us a dozen apples and get paid for a dozen and a half.
	"We'd much rather pay you $18 million *with* the Tiger name as agreed. But this proposal is a last-ditch attempt to make this deal work."

This approach may (or may not) succeed.

To the plus side Buyer may end up buying an asset that is ("less or less") what it wanted to buy. Without the Tiger name, the business being acquired really *is* objectively less valuable. The offsetting fact is that at a much lower re-calibrated price the aggregate transaction is financially attractive.

Risk and reward symmetry have been restored.

The lower the purchase price Buyer initially offers on this follow-up bargaining, the more latitude Buyer has to either slowly increase the purchase price during this second negotiation or make the second offer final and irrevocable.

Hearing $12 million should shock Seller. Maybe even *shell*-shock.

To some small degree the Tiger Family has already processed that they didn't sell the company. Inside their heads, however, they still believe they own a company worth $18 million. After all the market validated that premise.

The new communication shatters that belief.

"What? We just lost *six million dollars*!" People hate losing one dollar significantly more than they enjoy winning one dollar. Fear of loss is powerful.

Some behavioral economists and social scientists estimate it takes anywhere from $2.30 to $5.00 of gain to make up for $1.00 of loss.

This follow-up negotiating sequence simultaneously accepts and confirms Seller's own logic about the emotional value of the Tiger name but turns the economic consequences on its head.

The more value Buyer attributes to the name, the more Buyer validates the Family's wisdom in retaining it.

If Seller retains such a valuable name, Buyer's purchase price has to go down by a matching amount. That's straight-forward math. Symmetry on the transactional teeter-totter.

The ultimate reality that the value to Seller is largely *emotional* doesn't mean that calculating the equivalent value to Seller shouldn't be *economic.*

Family is family. Blood is blood. Cash is cash.

Solving every monetary issue doesn't necessarily resolve emotional or non-economic issues. Cash isn't the only form of transactional currency.

Chapter 3 Key Takeaways

- *All Deals are personal but Founders are more so.*

Money is always necessary to persuade and motivate a seller to sell, but money alone may not be sufficient. Founder emotion, ego, or fear of loss, identity, or power can trump economics and derail a deal.

People *hate* change and uncertainty. Who will they be? Where will they go the day after Closing?

One possible workaround is creating an important sounding corporate role for Seller. An impressive title with no authority. Give them an office … far, far away from headquarters.

Capture your counterparty's heart and their mind will follow. Or don't. They won't.

- **Exit broken deals the right way. Complain to your partners, not your counterparties.**

Deal lawyers and investment bankers have more than one client. You're likely to interact with some DealCirclers again. Nothing is gained by slamming the door behind you.

Even if you grit your teeth, send notes to everyone thanking them for their efforts. "Sorry things didn't work out, but we really appreciate your good faith assistance and great sense of humor."

Always leave them laughing. It's surprising how many times a deal that has seemingly died is resurrected at a later date with the same stage full of characters. You'd like them to welcome your entrance with a smile.

A HOUSE DIVIDED AGAINST ITSELF CAN'T BE BOUGHT

As we observed with the Reluctant Spouse in Tiger Tights, when privately held businesses (family or otherwise) are "for sale" all stockholders may not be wholly aligned for a medley of reasons.

- There may be less-than-100% *inclination* to sell, or
- There's agreement about *advisability* of selling but no explicit agreement to sell at (or above) a particular price.

Because those differences starkly impact a buyer's tactical approach and value proposition to seller, they're worth exploring in a non-family setting. A deal some years later with a Florence's Fashions–type industry buyer (Perennial Purchaser) had a happier ending.

In reaching agreement on purchase price and structure to acquire a closely held (but not family) business (Splintered Stone), we talked exclusively with its highly capable, enthusiastic CEO. Our understanding was he owned a majority (or at least a controlling interest) in Seller.

Splintered had been started ten years earlier. Most of the initial capital came from management and employees, but a minority was provided by silent, outside investors.

Unaware of the capital structure and source of funds, Buyer's experienced acquisition team believed the CEO was the sole Deal-Circler we'd have to persuade. All others on the sell-side would accede to the CEO's recommendation. We needed a single "yes" to trigger all necessary "yesses."

SPOILER ALERT. Bozo is about to make the same mistake ... again. Can you *believe* it?

Turns out we heard the wrong story, plot, and cast. Not even the wrong chapter; we misread the whole book, starting (once again) with misunderstanding who the decision-maker was.

Employee-stockholders we perceived as mere "extras" on this set had leading roles.

How did this epiphany occur?

- Brilliant introspective analysis? *No.*
- Announcement from lawyers the day before Closing? *No.*

Much less dramatic.

Earlier-than-normal in a transaction, Splintered Stone's CEO let me read the minutes of stockholder and director meetings. Not usually enthralling.

They rapidly became *heart-pounding.* At the stockholder meeting discussing a potential sale of the business, each stockholder's vote (and the stated reason for their vote) was recorded individually. I've never seen minutes like this before or since.

INDUSTRY TIP: *Not* recommended governance process.

Knowledgeable buyers scour corporate minutes looking for:

- unusual past events Buyer should be concerned about,
- confirmation all corporate formalities have been observed (e.g., electing directors and officers, authorizing stock option plans and grants, or approving terms of loans or equity financings), or
- information in conflict with the company's financial statements or footnotes.

Why? Information is power, and nuances matter. Every imperfection uncovered gives Buyer another basis for suggesting that the already-negotiated purchase price is too high, i.e., it was negotiated without knowledge of the imperfection.

The big reveal was only 51 stockholder votes favored a sale while 49 votes were opposed. Not a stampede to sell.

Seller's dangerous ploy in not alerting us to this?

If Buyer discovers any bad fact during its diligence process, Buyer becomes less trusting of anything else Seller has told them (and will tell them) about the business. Jerry Garcia put it better than I can: "Stuff that's hidden and murky and ambiguous is scary because you don't know what it does."

The result?

Like Sellers, Buyers also value certainty. They want certainty they're acquiring the business as it's being presented by Seller, and that nothing has been concealed from them. After unpleasant surprise discoveries most buyers seek a higher level of contractual and economic protection than they otherwise would have.

Seller's failure (intentional or inadvertent) to disclose his tenuous level of control dramatically decreased deal probability.

To give you a heads up (and permission to *not* study the detailed composite stockholder voting chart below), the actual reason for each stockholder's vote uniformly reflected their personal self-interest.

Their stated reason sounded statesmanlike (concern for the group as a whole) which by the sheerest of coincidences happened to align precisely with their personal self-interest.

Who would have guessed? Gambling in Casablanca!

Stock-holder	# of Shares	For or Against	*Stated* Reason	*Actual* Reason
Jill (Employee)	43	*For*	"They're a really good company. "We're too small to stay competitive by ourselves. "We need to join forces with a national business to survive."	"I'm irreplaceable and will get a raise. "They have a better 401K plan than we do."
Juanita (Non-Employee investor)	8	*For*	"It's a great price. "We should sell *now*. This is the perfect time to maximize our value."	"I've been in this deal for 12 years. Without a sale I'm never going to get out. "I don't care what the price is as long as I get liquid."
Logan (Employee)	25	*Against*	"This *isn't* the right time to sell. "We'll be worth more next year."	"I'm Director of Finance. No company needs two people heading their financial department. "After a sale I'll be demoted to a Controller (at best) or fired (at worst). "I'm really scared."
Atticus (Employee)	24	*Against*	"The price is clearly too low. They need us desperately. "Shouldn't we get other strategic buyers to bid against them and create competition?"	"I helped found this company, and I'm retiring in 2 years." "If we're independent, I'll work something out to keep my health insurance benefits. "If we're sold, I can't. That's bad for me and my family."

A meaningful amount of Splintered Stone's stock was owned by outside parties like Juanita. She'd invested many years earlier when Splintered Stone was a startup. Like the other non-affiliated stockholders, her decision to sell or not was entirely financial.

The balance of stock, however, was still held by *employees* who (like Jill and the CEO) had been with the company from inception. Non-management-employee-stockholders we assumed were *extras* (not shaping a corporate decision in their capacity as *employees*), had leading roles in this off-off-off-Broadway melodrama in their capacity as *voting stockholder-owners*.

The desire to sell couldn't have been less overwhelming or more ambivalent. Half the stockholders were motivated sellers. Half were neither willing nor motivated. All understandable as soon as you understood who they were, their position in the DealCircle, and the basis for their analysis.

Selling any company changes *who* makes corporate decisions and *how* and *when* they do so, savagely rocking the business boat. Following a change-of-control, roles and responsibilities for corporate "pioneers" get re-examined antiseptically by strangers not bound by emotional corporate history or memory.

Early employees often take personal risks to help start the business, give up good jobs at financially secure companies, and accept below-market cash salaries in exchange for stock in the company.

Any later transition in company ownership is scary and creates fear and uncertainty. Until then they felt safely ensconced in a special, protected category. They wouldn't fire themselves or adjust their positions.

The votes explained the otherwise inexplicable delaying/unresponsive behavior of a key senior manager who had slow-walked us through diligence and document exchange. She voted against the sale and was making a transaction as difficult as possible. Deliberately creating *considerable* friction where there shouldn't be *any* friction.

The deal was significantly less committed and solid than we had thought. Time to re-analyze Buyer and Seller's comparative leverage, change tactics to reflect new facts, and sing a different tune.

Leverage frequently shifts between counterparties as deals become increasingly detailed. Parties more accurately assess what they will gain or lose if the transaction closes. A "once-*willing* seller" becomes a *motivated* seller. A "once-*willing* buyer" sees more latent upside and becomes a *motivated* buyer.

Or the opposite.

A once-willing buyer stops being willing and moves on. You learn more on a second date (the diligence process) than a first (swipe right), and may not have any interest in a third.

We stopped behaving in buying mode, acting as if our counterparty was a motivated Seller. Our tactics assumed negotiating leverage was ours because Seller was already smelling the money.

We returned to *selling* mode; trying to persuade and entice the stockholders to want to accept our money. A 180-degree tactical reversal.

> **MILITARY AXIOM:** "No battle plan survives first contact with the enemy."

As a legal matter, the intended acquisition-by-merger technically requires only the slim majority stockholder approval we had. Other practical and legal considerations combine, however, so most Buyers (including us) won't merge without at least 90% approval. We were far from satisfying that real-world threshold.

Instead of pushing aggressively to improve the transaction (i.e., lower purchase price or further limit Buyer's financial exposure), we laser-focused on *closing* the deal on its current terms, wooing the now-identified reluctant stockholders to vote to sell.

We adjusted our negotiating filter by letting small economic "asks" move in Seller's favor, and not pursuing minor questions raised in diligence.

After identifying stockholders favoring the transaction, Buyer further solidified their intention to sell. Simultaneously we focused on changing the hearts, minds, and votes of stockholders *not* favoring the deal.

We approached "no" voting stockholders (particularly management or employees) to enthusiastically explain how *good* life would be for them with Buyer.

> **Buyer:** "After the deal closes we'll promote you from Purchasing Manager to Global Head of Asset Acquisition."
>
> Or …
>
> "You're so valuable we're offering you:
>
> - a three-year, guaranteed employment agreement at a higher salary *plus*
>
> - substantial noncompetition fees now, *plus*
>
> - a new, more important operating function and prestigious title.
>
> "Won't that be better for you than your current status as an employee-at-will who could be fired at any time?"

Increased their rewards. Decreased their risks. Usually a winning combination.

We also dramatically sped up negotiations to decrease time available for any "yes" stockholders to change their minds. It worked. None did. Even better, almost all "no" votes turned to "yes" and we completed what became a highly profitable acquisition.

Without reading the minutes this deal would probably have simply stalled from "invisible-to-us" internal non-alignment. Buyer would never have engaged with dissenting employee-stockholders who weren't part of Seller's negotiating team. They weren't in our line of sight; invisible DealCirclers.

Is your takeaway that these internal dynamics were matters we would never have known if we hadn't done the unusual and read the minutes?

Really?

NBA broadcasters (and tennis pros) call our tactical process an "unforced error."

Big difference between whether something is *unknown* or *unknowable*. Posing basic questions when budding acquisitions begin would have prevented this and made the dissenters a *known* problem we had to contend with.

- "*Who* controls stockholder votes needed to sell as a legal matter?"
- "*What* votes do you own personally or control as a practical matter?"
- "Do all *stake*holders (not *stock*holders) favor the transaction? Any negatives? *Why?*"

Normally we asked all those questions. Here we asked none.

An Expectation Unarticulated is a Disappointment Guaranteed.

CEO's behavior and status matched our expectations, so we never questioned them. Confirmation bias strikes again and extracts a heavy toll.

Dealing with two Co-Founders is five times harder than dealing with a single Founder, or "breaking up is hard to do."

Two Co-Founders had been the closest of friends and great business partners for 40 years before a financial impasse caused a bitter breaking point. They had to divide what would be a billion dollars today: $500 million each.

After several negotiating sessions, agreement was reached on separating ownership of dozens of buildings and operating businesses.

The only remaining issue? Who would receive the prime parking space located closest to the single office building they would still jointly own after the deal closed?

Unlike midtown Manhattan (where parking spaces can be valued like gold), a comparable space in a Midwestern suburb had *no* financial value. Despite that neither would give and let the other one have it.

I truly wish that were an exaggeration.

These types of highly emotional, completely non-economic, sticking points happen routinely in marital divorces ("The espresso machine is *mine!*"). It happens just as often in corporate divorces.

The deal floundered (or should I say "foundered"?) for months. The "sophisticated" back and forth repartee resembled the following.

Co-Founder #1: *"I'm* entitled to the parking space. It was my idea to buy this building from Nigel."

Co-Founder #2: *"I'm* entitled. I handled all the purchase negotiations and delicate financing. You never could have gotten it done without me. Nigel's a jerk."

Lawyers (for each Co-Founder): "Guys. Guys. Guys. Can't we all just get along? It's a parking space, not the Taj Mahal."

A Solomon-like solution was called for, but the parking space couldn't be split into two anymore than the biblical baby could. Neither Co-Founder was ever going to give the other the satisfaction of winning a battle over such a prime piece of "property."

How do you solve an unsolvable problem?

Everyone ultimately agreed to bulldoze the parking space out of existence. Destroy it. No one could use or own a parking space that didn't exist. Nothing left to fight over.

Neither Co-Founder was *happy* with this solution. Neither was so *unhappy* they were unwilling to close. Economic and emotional equilibrium had been achieved. We needed closure, not ecstasy.

Fortunately, their corporate name didn't include the name of either Co-Founder or we might never have completed this transaction!

On to the next escapade and a peek behind a different theater curtain: corporate finance in the land of troubled businesses.

Chapter 4 Key Takeaways

- Every deal is *fact-intensive* and *human-clay-specific*. Make sure you're hearing the right story from the real cast.

Don't jump to conclusions or assumptions. You don't have to be brilliant or clairvoyant. Ask for information directly and politely. Candor produces clarity.

Who has a stake in this deal's outcome? *What* gives them their power? *How* much do they have?

When counterparty responses correspond with their self-interest, your confidence level in their accuracy and veracity should increase.

- Don't get locked into a single view of any deal. There's more than one desired (or desirable) outcome. Adjust tactics and goals as facts (good or bad) emerge.

Deals aren't static. At any given moment negotiating leverage between the counterparties ebbs and flows back and forth on a transactional rollercoaster.

Intermittently step back and assess. Who wants the deal more *right now*? You? Your counterparty? What (if anything) does that change?

When *they* want the deal more, *you* gain leverage. When *you* do, *they* gain leverage. Your negotiating approach should reflect that first principle understanding.

THIS WASN'T MY FIRST RODEO. WHERE'S THE PONY?

My baptism under financial-distress-fire occurred during a deep national recession.

A talented business crisis consultant and I were out-of-town working all day to see if anything could be salvaged for our mutual client, a rapidly failing business. Flying home that night the following back-and-forth occurred:

> **Me:** "How can you possibly do this for a living? We just spent ten hours in an overheated, windowless conference room filled beyond capacity with people who are angry, unhappy, scared, in denial, dysfunctional, or all five. This is agony. I'm *exhausted*."

> **Crisis consultant** (looking at me with genuine bewilderment): "*Wow*, that's not how I see it at all. Every room I go into is covered with pony poop. **My job is to find the pony.**"

Simple words. Colorful metaphor. A lesson learned that cannot be improved upon.

No matter how troubled or unlikely a deal seems at any given moment, a Dealjammer's job is always to find the pony. Lemons only turn into lemonade if you squeeze hard enough and add sweetener. There's no spontaneous combustion.

That wisdom became a reflexive part of my thought process and reaction to virtually all circumstances in negotiating or life. Where's the pony?

In the two days of buying four companies from Paul's Parts, the negotiating environment was unquestionably intense. The company's *circumstances,* however, were as distant from a distressed sale as possible. The DealCircle about as small as possible. A Dealjammer's delight. No need to search for a pony.

Why?

Paul's Parts had:

- a sole-owner Seller,

- a solo lawyer, and

- an experienced Buyer whose decision-makers were physically present.

The DealCircle was small and obvious. Third parties were a nonfactor. No lender, landlord, or regulatory approval required.

There was no need for Paul's Parts CEO to invoke the "Seller's Mantra"—my shorthand vocabulary for the phrase every Seller should strive for and invoke repeatedly in every discussion with Buyer.

As a Seller I need:

Certainty about the outcome and consequences from each deal variable, and

Confidentiality about even the possibility of a transaction occurring. Complete confidentiality.

Those seller requirements were baked into the rules of Paul's Parts deal.

Neither was raised explicitly because it was inherently solved for.

The interval between starting and Closing was so short that as a practical matter neither counterparty was concerned about maintaining confidentiality. No one in the DealCircle even left the negotiating room.

Every deal element was crystal clear and provided certainty to Paul. He explicitly spelled out his conditions.

No uncertainty about if (or when) the deal would close.	Thursday or not at all.
No uncertainty about what financial reward Seller would receive.	All cash at Closing.
No uncertainty about Seller's financial exposure to Buyer after Closing.	No DealDebt, no holdbacks, no escrow, no future performance-based payments.

The extreme opposite deal environment exists when distressed businesses are involved. The obvious stakeholder-owners are severely threatened, and may have differing financial consequences and views, not dissimilar to Splintered Stone's 51-49 stockholders.

The DealCircle flexes. Customers, suppliers, lenders, and employees emerge from the stage's wings. They're each adversely impacted by Seller's cash difficulties and have a stake in the process and outcome.

Unsurprisingly, more people and legal specialists are involved in a $1 billion transaction in a highly regulated industry than the sale of a corner grocery store.

Behind the visible, negotiating corporate law partner who is easily identifiable in the DealCircle (and associates assisting her) there are a multitude of other lawyers from different disciplines: tax, pension, environmental, antitrust, labor, and/or intellectual property.

In a distressed sale, the most prominent addition is a bankruptcy/creditor's rights lawyer.

READER ASIDE: Buying a failing business like Impala in the following story is littered with important technical, legal, and financial issues mercifully beyond the scope of this book. You're encouraged to learn them elsewhere. We'll keep focusing on people, persuasion, and tactical perspectives.

Complexities abound, in part because more stakeholders are involved in selling a financially troubled business *with* bank debt than a profitable company *without* bank debt.

Deal obstacles get even harder to resolve if the distressed business is "Founder-formed" and still "Family-owned."

Tangled psychological and economic issues surface. Parent-child conflict or sibling rivalries impact negotiating dynamics. Intra-Family grievances present themselves as unconstructive barriers on seemingly irrelevant corporate issues.

It reminds me of a Chinese proverb: "You can always see the [corporate] carpet, but you can't always see the tigers fighting underneath the carpet."

Spotting the pony (or the Tiger) gets geometrically harder in distressed family transactions.

My client (Acquisitions R Us) was one of several bidders in what amounted to an informal auction to acquire an insolvent company (let's call them Impala Industries) outside of a bankruptcy court.

Although Impala's annual revenues were hundreds of millions of dollars, the disintegration of their business (combined with pressure from their corporate lender) made the purchase price range comparatively low.

They got started six decades earlier. The Founder-entrepreneur still retained a title (Chairman Emeritus) but (thanks to the miracles of sophisticated trust and estate planning) no stock.

The saga of a less-than-stellar second generation was not unfamiliar. The business was now wholly owned and managed (or more accurately, *mis*managed) by the next family generation. They graphically illustrated a foundational Maxim: ***Being a Founder (or a Founder's family) is a fact; not a job description.***

In an academic clinical medical setting, doctors talk about how an extremely sick patient "presents" (exhibits) an extraordinary number of symptoms. Really interesting for medical professionals to study and diagnose. Issues are voluminous, creating innumerable chances for blunder or brilliance.

Welcome to the Impala Institute for Ailing and Infirm Businesses. A full panoply of DealCirclers presenting us with a wide array of challenges.

The company was near bankruptcy and full-tilt-boogie losing its cash, credit, and customers. Sales and revenues had shrunk but operations and expenses hadn't. The Founder's family was rapidly losing their increasingly tenuous corporate control.

Impala's operating cash came largely from a substantial corporate loan, long since in default. (While not entirely fair, let's call their lender "Big Bad Bank.") If the loan wasn't repaid, Big Bad Bank had the normal rights and remedies of most secured lenders.

The bank could seize and sell all *collateral*. Those are assets owned by borrower and "pledged" to a bank to secure a loan. (If a pawn shop isn't repaid, the shop can sell the pawned object and apply the proceeds to the loan.)

In this case, Impala owned (and had pledged) its inventory, customer receivables, equipment, manufacturing facilities, and related real property to Big Bad Bank.

Impala's corporate loan was additionally buttressed by personal guarantees from Family members. (If Impala didn't repay the loan, Family Guarantors would write the checks that would.)

With good reason, Big Bad Bank had tried repeatedly to force the Family to face hard truths about Impala's declining future, the imperative need to drastically cut management salaries and corporate costs, and the impending need to sell the business.

Time passed. No change in corporate behavior. The bank accurately assessed that the Family was operating under the mistaken belief that looming loan default and foreclosure were the *bank's* problem alone rather than a shared problem that strongly included them.

Geographically the Impala Family was in the State of Montana. Psychologically they were in the increasingly populous State of Denial. Its Capital? Dysfunction.

Denial is a well-known human defensive coping mechanism. In the face of uncomfortable facts ("you're going to run out of money"), people unconsciously more than consciously avoid thinking about (or accepting the reality of) unbearable news or information.

Denial leads to rejecting overwhelming objective evidence because acceptance is too emotionally painful. Complicates negotiating at a cosmic level.

Dealjammers and lenders have interacted with citizens from the State of Denial more times than they would have preferred. They recognize its citizens and their symptoms.

Impala's increasingly frustrated "relationship banker" sharply pierced Borrower's denial by summarizing the financial exposure of individual Family members.

> **Banker** "The Credit Committee asked me to re-
> (to Family): mind you that Family members Misha, Sandor, and Pasha 'jointly and severally' guaranteed Impala's Loan.
>
> "If our loan isn't fully repaid, our 'work-out team' will let you know the precise amount you need to pay individually for any 'shortfall.'
>
> "That's bank lingo for any amount we don't receive from everything Impala owes us for the loan's principal, interest, default penalties, late fees, and our attorney's fees."

Family members who appeared to have been dozing and bored suddenly became deeply engaged.

> **Misha:** "I only own 15% of Impala's stock. It's not fair for me to owe 100% of the shortfall!"

Bank: "It may or may not be *fair*, but it's *accurate*. That's what 'jointly and severally' means.

"Without your personal guarantees the Credit Committee wouldn't have approved Impala's corporate credit. As *individuals*, you're collectible. As a *corporation*, Impala isn't.

"Respectfully, how you allocate financial obligations among yourselves is your Family's decision, not the bank's decision."

READER ASIDE: Banks don't always enforce or collect on guarantees. The *threat* of enforcement and collection, however, is powerful. Lenders' financial, legal, and emotional leverage impacts borrower's behavior and encourages cooperation.

Guarantors' vulnerability as *individuals* makes them more susceptible to sweet reason about resolving *corporate* matters. Loan defaults change from an abstract, impersonal *bank's* problem to an intensely personal, *individual* problem.

What's the difference?

Maybe an old joke illustrates the delta between how people experience *impersonal* sets of circumstances compared with *personal*.

Question: What's the difference between a *recession* and a *depression*?

Answer: A *recession* is when *many* people are out of work. A *depression* is when *you're* out of work.

Big Bad Bank threatened to stop funding and put Impala into formal bankruptcy court proceedings unless the Family agreed to sell the business right now. In court, the Family would almost certainly lose everything. Banks might not always enforce guarantees but bankruptcy judges and creditors tend to be less forgiving.

The corporate collateral still retained value. It was borderline, but the loan might be repaid in full if Impala were sold as an ongoing business outside of a bankruptcy shutdown.

That fact-of-life "transmogrified" (See, *Calvin and Hobbes*) the Big Bad Bank into the unmistakable deal driver in this DealCircle (not the Family). All meaningful negotiating leverage rested in lender hands.

Normally selling Impala would have been led by the bank's "workout" department (not people you want to know first-hand), or by retaining a professional investment banker.

With explicit approval of Big Bad Bank, Impala's sales efforts were spearheaded by the Family Advisor, an unusual choice. No matter how promising or talented, rookie quarterbacks make more unforced errors than veterans.

On the *plus* side, she was the trusted investment and financial wizard for multiple Impala generations.

On the *minus* side, she had no deal experience.

Some reward. Some risk.

What made her a solid choice was in-depth understanding of Family dynamics. Her voice would be heard (and advice trusted) by all. This was super important in emotionally charged circumstances where internecine squabbling could derail an otherwise sensible outcome.

Family Advisor knew her clients and understood their emotional and financial vulnerability. They were desperate for any corporate-level solution in which they didn't individually have to pay money as guarantors, and potentially go into bankruptcy personally.

She played the cards as dealt, but it's hard to imagine a shakier hand. No leverage against Big Bad Bank. As weak a negotiating position as imaginable with plausible acquirors.

A well-conceived part of her tactical plan emerged: keeping likely buyers far, far away from the Family. No bidders were allowed to directly communicate with them. Divide and conquer strategies weren't going to happen on her watch.

The only viable buyers were industry strategic buyers (like us) looking to expand their geographic footprint and increase and diversify their customer base.

None would be excited by Impala's aging plant or easily replaceable inventory or equipment. None would see value in Seller's senior management/Family members. (It wasn't a trade secret why Seller was insolvent).

All strategics had similar motivations and could:

- quickly evaluate the financial value of Seller's inventory, customers, sales force, physical locations, and branded names,
- manage Seller's business if acquired, and
- increase their own revenues and profit by buying Impala.

Family Advisor had already gauged interest in a slew of strategics with a fill-in-the-blank (two-page), non-binding Letter of Intent (LOI). Little was called for other than interested bidders inserting their proposed purchase price confirming their interest in buying Impala in the vaguest of terms.

Like everyone else, we executed and returned the LOI. Signing cost and committed us to nothing other than maintaining confidentiality and kept us in the buying-negotiating mix.

What's not to like?

Presumably Family Advisor's goal was identifying the maximum number of meaningful bidders. Then slowly reduce bidding to a handful of companies and play them against each other.

That's a terrific strategy in a stable set of circumstances. However, this was closer to a corporate-car-crash-in-waiting.

Sophisticated Sellers typically push hard for longer, more detailed letters of intent (closer to eight pages than two). In addition to *major* economic terms (price and payment) as importantly they delineate minor terms (less obviously financially impactful) provisions.

Seller's full economic cost and exposure from these *minor* details may not be obvious on their face:

- *amount* of purchase price "deferred," i.e., not paid to Seller at Closing and handled through escrows, notes, or holdbacks,

- *scope* of Seller's representations and warranties, and

- *limitations* on Seller's indemnification obligations, i.e., what's Seller's maximum financial exposure (in dollars) and how long can Buyer make claims against Seller?

Purchase price *deferred* may be purchase price *denied.*

The more Seller's representations are *un*qualified and categorical (every receivable *will be* collected) the greater the probability that some will be inaccurate.

That's why Sellers want their representations to be as *highly* qualified as possible. ("To the best of my conscious knowledge, with absolutely no inquiry whatsoever, every account receivable absolutely *might be* collectible … maybe).

The longer the indemnification period, the more likely Seller will owe Buyer money for breach of those representations.

The consequence?

Sellers want the:

- fewest possible *representations,*

- most *qualifications* to the reps they do make,

- shortest *indemnification period* for violating those reps, and

- lowest indemnification *"cap,"* i.e., the maximum amount Seller will owe Buyer regardless of the amount of economic damage Buyer incurs.

In a short-form LOI, these provisions are frequently omitted. Buyers casually dismiss them by saying those minor issues will be contained in the "definitive deal documents." Details will be on "customary terms and conditions for these kinds of transactions."

Question: Why is this a giant, flashing red light?

Answer: Selling a business *isn't* like selling a house.

Home-selling DealCirclers probably *do* have a strong sense of what "customary terms and conditions" mean. Business buyers and sellers *don't*.

There are boatloads of comparable residential transactions (lots about *lots*). Definitive deal documents (transfer documents and deeds) are publicly recorded and available for review. What constitutes customary terms and conditions may vary slightly region-by-region, but tend to be understood by all *within* each region.

Most states have standard forms for residential sales identifying home Buyer, Seller, their attorneys, property being sold, and approximate lot size. Usually there is a specific addenda where Buyer and Seller can mutually modify the norm, or add particular agreements not contemplated by the form.

The words used in residential sales are familiar to most of us and available to all.

More significantly, real estate agents for home Buyer and Seller would probably largely agree on what they mean. Even a first-time home buyer will receive information from their intermediary enabling them to understand the transaction and make informed choices.

To make this comparison clearer, let's take a quick peek at a standard home sale agreement as a reference point to illuminate the mischief that can be unleashed if the corporate short-form LOI primarily details only the purchase price.

Because of the detail provided in the residential purchase-and-sale agreement, buyers and sellers can calculate the actual net amount they will pay or receive in the transaction. The net reflects *all* agreed-to economic adjustments to the stated purchase price.

If drapes are *excluded* from the purchase, Buyer will have to pay for new drapes, increasing Buyer's actual purchase price. If they're *included*, Buyer has no added cost.

Home seller and buyer also allocate risks for pre-Closing conditions and post-Closing conditions.

STANDARD FORM CONTRACT FOR PURCHASE AND SALE OF A RESIDENCE

What is Home Buyer purchasing

Buyer's and Seller's legal names.

Description of the property.

Are items located at the property included or excluded?

Included:
- Washer and dryer,
- Refrigerator

Excluded:
- Drapes
- Chandelier

Who pays for

Closing costs.

Mortgage expense and recording fees.

Required title survey.

Transfer taxes.

Real estate brokers fees.

Diligence and Closing conditions

Condition of premises (i.e., seller's factual representations about the asset being sold).

Title survey and insurance. Which conditions will affect title?

Home Buyer's right of inspection:
- structural,
- pests,
- septic systems,
- radon

Mortgage contingency

Transfer document is a **Warranty Deed** with a Lien Covenant

Merger and acquisition (M&A) deals are similar with respect to purchase price, economic adjustments, and risk allocation but with more extensive and dramatic consequences.

Negotiating leverage for business sellers peaks while negotiating the Letter of Intent, *not* while negotiating the definitive documents. Before the LOI is signed, Seller isn't contractually obligated to sell, and is free to talk to other buyers.

The threat of no deal and the threat of competition to Buyer is real. As soon as the LOI is signed granting bidder exclusive rights to negotiate a transaction with Seller for the specified time duration (commonly 30–60 days), negotiating leverage shifts strongly to Buyer.

The company is now off-the-market. No one else can purchase Seller unless/until Buyer and Seller fail to reach agreement and don't close.

If you're looking to buy a house, how do you react to seeing a "Sale pending" sign in front of a house? Most folks reasonably assume there's a contract to sell the house, and the sale will close soon. The house isn't available for them to purchase.

They drive right by (in the analog world) or flip to the next image of houses for sale (in the digital). No one but the buyer-under-contract displays any interest in purchasing the house.

The same phenomenon exists in M&A transactions but maybe even more so. There's no *"sale pending"* sign on seller's corporate front lawn, but there's also no *"for sale"* sign. That's what signing the LOI does (whether two or eight pages).

Seller now has to stop all outbound selling efforts. If there are any residual *inbound* inquiries, the LOI-bound Seller is contractually prohibited from responding. Seller loses all market momentum and potential competitive pressures from other possible bidders.

Buyer's lawyers prepare extensive definitive documentation whose "customary terms and conditions" skew heavily in Buyer's favor. They have considerable latitude because there are no authoritative guidelines for what "customary" means. Unburdened by boundaries, document producers may act as if customary is a synonym for "incendiary."

The bottom line?

As negotiations continue, the documents and terms get more favorable to Buyer and less favorable to Seller. Buyer-friendly deal creep. More risk gets allocated to Seller. Concepts Seller would never have agreed to on "Day-LOI" become embedded by "Day-Closing."

Risk increases. Reward decreases.

Seller's vulnerability prompted my conclusion that ***The Seller's Mantra is Certainty and Confidentiality.***

(We touched lightly on this earlier, and the theme will crop up often in Dealjammer chronicles.)

Using the Seller's Mantra as a negotiating prism is the key to:

- identifying, recognizing, and articulating Seller's most critical needs,
- maximizing Seller's price, and
- minimizing Seller's risk of loss.

Applied consistently and correctly it creates tactical and strategic advantages. Every seller, whether voluntary (like prosperous Paul's Parts) or forced (like financially distressed Impala), should look for and value certainty that:

- negotiations remain totally *confidential,*
- the *deal will close* on the LOI-agreed-to economic terms (major *and* minor),
- Seller *will get paid* what they expect to be paid *when* they expect to be paid, *plus*
- Seller's *financial exposure* after Closing (to Buyer or others) is limited in time and amount so Seller can keep what they get paid.

The drone of the Seller's Mantra (the Maxim's Anthem), should be enunciated early and often, a relentless chant and intonation, chorus and refrain, and finally to a prolonged, deep, reverberating sound and demand. Elevates the words *Certainty* and *Confidentiality* from a useful catch phrase to a hymn:

- a mere *concept* that Seller tentatively "raised" ("I thought I'd *mention* it") transforms into,

- an implacable, tangible *demand* that *must* be dealt with ("I *have* to have it").

Meanwhile, back in Impala-land, nothing advanced toward a transaction. Jiggling in "DealJello."

As a result of Family Advisor's widespread outreach, confidentiality had already been shattered. The entire industry knew Impala was for sale. Too late for Impala to demand something already lost by their own actions.

Not true for *certainty*.

The Family Advisor's plan of attack valued potentially competitive pricing pressure more highly than certainty of a Closing as soon as possible.

Not dissimilar to a homeowner incorrectly assessing that it was a seller's real estate market, trying to trigger competitive bids above the asking price, when it was actually a buyer's market.

The strategic trade-off may not have worked to Seller's advantage. It implicitly assumed all buyers were equally capable of closing a transaction, making purchase price the sole differentiator among bidders.

Not necessarily a good assumption.

For owners like Impala, the impending transaction is an exit, the end of their relationship with the company.

For customers, suppliers, and employees it's simultaneously the *end* of an existing relationship with Owner-Seller, and the *beginning* (or not) of a new one with Buyer. For good reason they have a negotiating voice and presence silent in Paul's Parts (with the single exception of Paul's talented SVP).

In a troubled DealCircle, many non-owners have a higher-than-normal negotiating profile, a visible stake in the business sale's outcome, and different self-interests than owners.

They worry about:

- receiving the money (or guaranteed work or services) distressed business already owes them, and
- *how* their future relationship and profitability will be impacted by the sale's outcome.

Following the Big Bad Bank's lead, suppliers were threatening to stop providing credit to Impala and only ship inventory on a cash basis, a prospective death knell.

Non-owners are watching this whole process from their own, unique perspective in the third concentric DealCircle. Suppliers may fear some bidders if they are known as cost-cutters or bad managers. If they're the winning bidder, suppliers' future profit margin or revenues will be reduced. Other bidders will be *favored* by suppliers as an improvement on existing owners and management.

The slow-moving informal auction process stretched an already heavily populated DealCircle to maximum size and human complexity.

Deteriorating external relationships were also damaging *internal* human assets.

Invaluable salespeople were threatening to leave. Competitors (including other bidders) were soliciting Impala's longtime customers to shift business to them, taking advantage of Impala's corporate instability and personnel insecurity.

I could clearly hear the train whistle blowing in the Grateful Dead's "Casey Jones," warning other railroaders that danger was coming. Would sell side DealCirclers heed the same warning and react?

Nero-the-fiddler was making music but meanwhile Rome was burning

Neither Bank nor Family Advisor changed course or speed.

Question: After sixty years in business what difference could a few more days in the sales process make?

Answer: All the difference in the world to us as Buyer.

The universe isn't static. As time passes deals unravel and facts change. (We'll explore this more later.) At some juncture acquisitions aren't worth pursuing. Re-test your original hypothesis.

> **Me** (to CEO): "Do you still want to buy Impala?

> **CEO:** "By month-end there's no reason to buy this business. The prize is Impala's sales force and customer base, which are both on the verge of imploding.
>
> "If we don't buy the company soon, we're better served picking off their customers and sales personnel one-by-one, and paying nothing for the privilege."

The CEO's sober analysis unriddled the limited choices.

> **Me:** "Then we either have to seize control of this gummed-up negotiating process and close quickly ...
>
> or
>
> "Abandon our efforts and stop wasting time, human resources, and money on a deal you no longer want."

Necessity is the Mother of Everything.

When a box you're operating in is rapidly shrinking, it's a good idea to think out of it. (Of course, as my wife Amy remarks, she'd be more impressed by my ability to think *out* of the box if she believed even for a second that I knew where the box *was*. Cruel, but not necessarily wrong.)

This deal-jam was going nowhere good. Could we modulate this faltering rhythm and tempo? Shift keys? Write new lyrics?

A novel incentive was imperative to jolt all decision-making stakeholders into action: Family, Big Bad Bank, customers, suppliers, and sales force.

The Seller's Mantra rang in my ears and sang from my mouth.

> **Me:** "We're indistinguishable from every bidder; submitting skimpy Letters of Intent slightly upping our purchase price offer. At this pivotal moment even submitting a super-lengthy Letter of Intent with full economic details is too slow.
>
> "What if we *demonstrated* certainty rather than just *talking* about certainty to convince them we should be the buyer-of-choice?
>
> "Let's draft *every* document needed to finalize this transaction with every counterparty (not just the Family), and provide them to all decision-makers *right now.*"

> **CEO** (ever practical): "I like it! How long will it take and what will it cost?"

> **Me:** "Two days to prepare. Hundreds of pages. A *humongous* legal fee; maybe ten times your normal monthly bill.
>
> "If we get the deal closed, you'll tell me the fee was cheap, and I'm a genius. If we don't, you'll tell me the fee was insanely expensive, and I'm an idiot."

Before daylight broke on Day Three we had prepared:

- 60+ page Acquisition Agreement (including exhibits), tailored specifically for Impala's DealCircle,

- Employment and Noncompetition Agreements,

- Big Bad Bank's Release of all collateral *plus* all Guarantors, and

- Opinion letter from Impala's law firm.

The full package was sent to the Big Bad Bank, Family Advisor, Family Lawyers, and Family Accountants, knowing they would collectively analyze and discuss with the Family.

What we *didn't* send was any change to our most recent purchase offer of $11.5 million, an amount fully repaying Impala's loan and other creditors but leaving nothing for the Family.

Buyer's deal team collaboratively composed the scripted song we were going to sing in *every* communication with *every* counterparty in this DealCircle. A libretto designed to fully satisfy the Seller's Mantra.

Lightly paraphrased it was:

> **Buyer:** "We're the *best* buyer and you should engage with us *exclusively*. Why? We're paying *all cash* at Closing." *Certainty*.
>
> "You don't have to guess what we want for representations or indemnification because you've read them." *Certainty*.
>
> "You have every Closing document. If you signed them *today* as presented, we could close and fund *tomorrow*." *Certainty*.
>
> "Unlike other bidders, we don't need approval from anyone outside our company or even our Board of Directors. We *will* close." *Certainty*.
>
> "Your customers, suppliers, and sales personnel will welcome us and stay. We're universally trusted after a dozen successful acquisitions." *Certainty*.
>
> "Put it all together and we have removed risk for all interested stakeholders." *Certainty*.
>
> "Other bidders? Maybe not so much." **Uncertainty.**

What we were offering directly to an increasingly motivated (but highly emotionally conflicted) Impala Family (and indirectly to their extremely financially motivated but emotionally *unconflicted* Bank) was a lifeboat of certainty in a sea of fear and uncertainty. The M&A equivalent of making an all-cash bid with no financing or inspection contingencies for a home.

Would you rather have a songbird in the hand (us) or two in the bush (everyone else)? That question is as close to rhetorical as I can make it.

How best to make the sale and seal this deal?

If it's important, do it in person.

This transaction wasn't just important to Impala's Family, it was existential.

For Buyer the opportunity was meaningful but *not* existential. The transaction was attractive only at the right price, terms, and timing. We were comfortable walking away.

Asymmetrical counterparty motivations and leverage favored us.

We enunciated our Rules of Engagement early and repeated them often to Family Advisor. (Echoing and repetition are important factors in imprinting the *Buyer's* Mantra.)

> **Buyer's CEO** (to Family Advisor): "If we reach 100% agreement by the end of a single, in-person, negotiating day, we have a deal. You'll immediately stop talking with other corporate suitors, engage exclusively with us, and we'll close in thirty days.
>
> "If we *don't* reach full agreement by five o'clock we'll wish you well and part ways as friends. Our flight departs at six thirty, and we'll be on it."

The full DealCircle met in Seller's city for a one-day negotiating session. Family Advisor's offices were full-to-overflowing with the extended Impala's Family, lawyers, and accountants. Their friendly banker was available via phone.

Our tactics were all about *framing*, *persuading*, and *closing*; collectively creating what consulting-speak describes as a "forcing function."

We needed all DealCircle decision-makers (and influencers) in the same space (at the same time) for the identical reason we needed both spouses present for an encyclopedia sale.

Leave no time or opportunity for second thoughts or Seller's Remorse from stakeholders not at the negotiating table. We wanted to look in the eyes of *all* counterparties and assess their body language and reactions.

DealCircling the proverbial wagons.

What we *didn't* want was Family Advisor shielding us from negotiating directly with the Family and further stringing out decision making.

Propinquity counts.

As physical proximity increases, the influence of others in the DealCircle recedes.

Faces you know are more important than faces you *don't* know. People you see are more important than people you *don't* see. The closer you are to someone physically, the more influenced you are by them and the more they're influenced by you. And vice versa.

It's such a fundamental premise of selling and negotiating that we'll come back to it several more times for thinking about different deals, tactics, and strategies.

Meanwhile, now that we truly were able to see everyone, back-and-forth bargaining about purchase price continued nonstop all day.

Family Advisor:	$28MM
Us:	*$11.5MM*
Family Advisor:	$27MM
Us:	*$11.5MM*
Family Advisor:	>$25MM
Us:	*$11.5MM*

Forty-five minutes before our five o'clock deadline Buyer's deal team left the room to compare observations and share intuitions.

Who on Impala's deal team had sweated? Whose eyebrows arched or shoulders shrugged when we made a point? Who nervously held their breath from tension?

Our collective inference was we knew the exact minimum price acceptable to all Impala's DealCircle decision-makers. The group gut speaking. Heart, not head. None of us could articulate precisely what we had observed, heard, or experienced to justify our level of conviction.

Fifteen minutes later (thirty minutes before our self-imposed five o'clock departure deadline) we re-entered the meeting.

With the CEO's blessing I delivered the following "speech-verging-on-sermon." By design it was deliberately calm, expressed in measured phrasing, and delivered in a conversational tone.

Firm. Unflappable. Immutable. *Not* threatening. *Not* belligerent.

I wasn't *selling*. I was *telling*.

> **Me:** "Here's our final offer:
>
> It's not $12.*8* million;
>
> It's not $12.*6* million
>
> It's not $12.*1* million;
>
> It's not even $12 million and fifty cents.
>
> It's *exactly* $12 million."
>
> "You're welcome to take it or leave it. Either way we're done negotiating. Accept our price and structure, sign an Exclusive with us now, or (as agreed) we're leaving for the airport in twenty-nine minutes."

My one-minute monologue had some elements of a musical crescendo, i.e., a gradual, steady increase in the loudness, force, or intensity of sound. I did *not* increase loudness, but I *did* deliberately increase my voice's force and intensity.

The cumulative effect is much different than if I had started by flatly stating that our offer is "$12 million."

Uttering only a single word ($12 million) lacks the dramatic arc of a series of descending words. Repetition creates a near-crescendo—wave after wave after financial wave crashing on Seller's shore.

Words and rhythm create a pattern. Each number is smaller than the one before. Listeners recognize patterns. They begin expecting each successive number to be smaller and smaller and smaller and smaller.

For all they knew, the last number was going to be *$11* million.

What a relief to Seller that the numbers stopped getting smaller and stopped on a number *larger* than our current $11.5 million offer.

An early mentor admonished me to "say what you mean, mean what you say, but never say what you say meanly."

We were all in the same room. We *meant* what we said. Impala Family and deal team could all *see, sense, feel,* and *hear* we meant it. With only the slightest imagination they could *taste* how close they were to financial salvation. Encyclopedia sale redux.

The exclusive was signed at 4:55 p.m. We closed three weeks later.

> **INDUSTRY TIP:** Like a Grateful Dead concert, the impact and value of in-person negotiations is three-dimensional and experiential, not easily captured in two-dimensional text or digital exchanges.

The most impactful Dealjamming occurs when all five senses are engaged through a face-to-face, flesh-to-flesh, intersection with *today's* audience, *today's* counterparties, *today's* DealCircle.

You can't smell fear or feel greed through digital exchanges, phone calls, or even Zoom.

You *can* gain these insights if (and only if) you're at the concert or in the room. We were in the room.

Being physically close with people counts.

READER ASIDE: Other speeches could have been delivered as Buyer's *final* message. Here are a few and why they weren't.

Buyer's Speech:	What Seller hears and how they respond:
"What would you say to $12 million?"	That's not a final *declaration*, it's a *question*. Seller can merely say "no"; or *counter* with "what would *you* say to *$25 million*"?
"We're increasing our offer by $500,000."	"*Great* first step. "Increase your offer by the same amount many more times, you'll get to $25 million, and we'll accept."

Another alternative is uncomplicated: "Our final offer is $12 million." These words definitely indicate finality. Substantively the same as what we actually said.

What *isn't* the same is *how* we said it. No words in this version *scream* finality.

Flat. Devoid of emotional power. Lacking the dramatic, theatrical impact of declining repetition.

If a counterparty daydreamed (or blinked or coughed) while I said, "our final offer is $12 million," they could easily miss the punchline. They're only five words. Two seconds.

If I:

- *mumbled* people wouldn't hear me because they *couldn't* hear me.

- *spoke too quickly* people wouldn't hear me because they *couldn't* hear me.

- talked as if I were reading from a written text, people wouldn't hear me because they *couldn't* hear me. (Writing and talking are totally different communication modalities.)

What we said and *how* we said it was designed to capture the undivided attention of all Impala stakeholders. No one in the DealCircle could emerge with even a glimmer of hope that our final offer wasn't our *final* offer.

They didn't. *Certainty.*

With Impala and several other closings under our belt, maybe now is a good time for a big picture view of the myriad subtle, serendipitous ways deals *start*, and the corporate cradles they rise from.

Chapter 5 Key Takeaways

Buying distressed businesses (outside of bankruptcy) is more complex legally and psychologically than other acquisitions.

- *Owners* face financial insecurity and devastating stress, routinely impairing their behavior (if not actively paralyzing them). Avoidance behavior and denial follow.

There are inevitably too many cooks in an emotionally overheated corporate kitchen. Legitimate agendas and interests of *non-owner* DealCirclers (customers, suppliers, employees, creditors) influence acceptable deal outcomes and have to be addressed. Otherwise you won't reach closure.

That reality makes it more important than normal to eliminate outside noise or influences by gathering all genuine *decision-makers* (not influencers) in a single room for a definitive negotiation. *"Propinquity counts."*

- ***"Deals, like the universe, tend toward entropy."*** That happens more quickly with troubled businesses than stable businesses because the to-be-acquired asset's value decays rapidly. Speed is imperative. Dealjammers should buy the company quickly or walk from the deal.

- After Closing, today's negotiating counterparties may be tomorrow's colleagues. What you say in heat-of-the-moment meetings impacts post-Closing relationships for years to come. Select your messages (and who you say them to) carefully.

You'll live with the consequences of:

- *What* you say,

- *How* you say it,

- The *tone* you *use*, and

- The *words* you *choose*.

DEALS DON'T START WITH A BIG BANG ... UNLESS THEY DO

Knowing how to initiate transactions may be as important for Dealjammers as knowing how to close them. All available evidence suggests that if a deal doesn't start, odds are extremely high (100%) it won't close.

Some physicists speculate our cosmos began as a Big Bang, a single moment and point in time which exploded and continuously expanded, resulting in today's stars and planets.

The scientific theory may or may not be valid, but the words provide a colorful framework and metaphor for thinking about the *"5 Ws"* of business deals*: who, what, where, when, why* (and sometimes *how*) transactions begin and the process and results that follow.

Selling encyclopedias started with knocking on a door and getting admitted to a house. (No small feat by itself.) Do deals also begin with an identifiable moment, an objective event, a Business Big Bang?

Looking through an exaggerated transactional telescope, every negotiation and sale of an asset involves not dissimilar processes, motivations, decision-making, and documents; always with some meaningful domain-specific "twists."

Before any negotiation begins, an asset (a "thing") is owned by a counterparty. A transaction ends when ownership has been transferred to someone else. The sequence and process have much in common whether the thing being sold is an encyclopedia, residence, shopping center, or business.

Different asset transfers involve different DealCirclers, knowledge, and variables.

We can still arbitrarily divide selling encyclopedias, homes, businesses, or shopping centers into four steps/phases:

- *presale* preparation,
- a Big Bang (or not),
- *negotiating*, and
- *due diligence* and *Closing documentation.*

Selling encyclopedias is the least complex process, with the smallest DealCircle, involving the fewest DealCirclers, and shortest timeframe from negotiation-start to sale-close. Maybe an hour.

Business acquisitions are the most complex, with the largest Deal-Circle, involving the most DealCirclers, and in general involving the longest time. Maybe weeks or months.

Functionally, however, the *sequence* of actions and processes are more alike than not.

More readers have some experience with buying or selling residences than encyclopedias, businesses, or office buildings. That's handy because the beginning of a residential sale *isn't* a cosmic mystery. Residences are either "*on* the market" (*for* sale) or "*off* the market" (*not* for sale).

Let's chart a residential sale through Four Phases as a common reference point for investigating corporate Big Bangs.

Echoing Crosby, Stills, Nash and Young's song, every seller believes their house is "a very, very, very, fine house." Everyone believes their house is the best on their block.

Humans focus selectively on what's bad about neighboring houses (very much), and what's good about theirs (much more). The predictable result is overrating the value of their own assets ("superiority bias"). No one hums the Grateful Dead's "Brokedown Palace."

STEP 1: Preparing for sale—the process	STEP 2: Big Bang	STEP 3: Negotiating; three different buying sequences	STEP 4: Closing: Papering the sale
Homeowner hires **real estate agent**. Conscious decision; active conduct.	**Agent** starts advertising online. Places a **"For Sale"** sign in front of house and lists the asking price.	**Potential buyer** *accepts* asking price; *no* negotiation.	**Standard pre-printed form contract**; little/ no negotiation except filling in Purchase Price on the standard form. (Like selling an encyclopedia.)
They collaboratively maximize home's **curb appeal,** e.g., paint/patch exterior, fix driveway cracks, install new kitchen cupboards.	Both are *conspicuous, unambiguous, readily observable* Big Bangs.	*Stable* real estate market. Buyers bid *below* asking price; triggering price negotiation.	Separately, agree on "minor" items (on customary terms). Level of inspection before Closing (diligence), move-in date, time to obtain mortgage financing, or who pays real estate transfer tax.
Like theater, they "stage" the house to best shape and frame the first impression of possible buyers.	Prospective buyers come to an Open House, tour the home, walk the neighborhood, and decide to bid (or not).	*Overheated* markets. Buyers bid *above* list price, competing against each other.	97% predictable.
		To distinguish themselves, Bidders offer cash with no financing contingency, hoping Seller accepts their bid.	
		Sales price *exceeds* asking price.	

Steps 1 and 2 for any sale (preparing to sell and a Big Bang announcing availability to purchase) require conscious action by Seller, easily observable for encyclopedias and houses alike.

Business deals don't necessarily arrive pre-packaged and easily observable. Some start with Big Bangs (*formal* sales process). Others don't (*informal* sales process).

Some deal *"whos"* and *"whats"*

Common business combinations occur between:

- suppliers and their major customers (*vertical* integrations),
- industry competitors (*horizontal* integrations), or
- large companies (Goliath) buying smaller companies (David).

That's the *who*.

Some of the *whats* are David's products, brands, or services. Goliath-Buyer can sell these to their existing customers through its larger, better developed sales and distribution channel. Goliath will sell more of David's products than David can, at least on DealDay-Closing. (We saw that business logic earlier in Paul's Parts.)

Formal sales of businesses

Some Deal *"when-do-they-starts"*

A business owner consciously decides to sell their business because they *have to* (financially distressed Impala) or are *willing* to (Paul's Parts). They retain an intermediary ("investment banker" for larger deals; "business broker" for smaller deals). Closely resembles Step 1 of a residential sale when homeowner/seller retains a real estate agent to run a process.

Investment banker and business owner tidy up Seller's corporate financial statements, books and records, and position the business as attractively as possible, (*Stage* the sale).

The Deal Big Bang occurs when:

- presale preparation work is finished,

- a "Confidential Information Memorandum" (effectively a selling brochure) disclosing key information about the business and its prospects has been created, and

- investment banker "goes to market," using the Memorandum to solicit prospective buyers.

These steps and phases in a *formal* process closely resemble selling encyclopedias *and* houses (intentionally ignoring notably different vocabulary and counterparties).

Informal sales of businesses

There are often no identifiable starting points for informal acquisitions of startups or privately held, entrepreneurial businesses. There is no *when*. No Big Bang. Deals emerge from myriad moments and bitesize buyer/seller interactions.

Some noted and obvious. Some not so much. Some start organically and unfold over months or years. Some are supercars accelerating from zero to sixty in 2.5 seconds.

Buying a company not explicitly for sale isn't like buying an encyclopedia or house. There is no fixed price. Businesses aren't cans of soup in the grocery store with uniform ingredients, size, weight, and shelf pricing.

There may not be an asking price or even an obvious *magnitude* of price. (Remember business owner wasn't planning to sell.) Any business is worth (its fair market value) only what a "ready, willing, and able" buyer will pay. That value varies wildly depending on what benefits Buyer believes they can derive by owning the asset.

Corporate beauty lies in the eyes of the specific corporate beholder.

Some Deal *"whys"*

Initial steps in the dating dance (mating dance?) between customer (corporate "buyer-in-waiting") and supplier ("seller-in-waiting") may look like this:

Step 1. Goliath-customer buys goods or services ("Stuff") from David-supplier.

Step 2. Supplier performs splendidly and David and Goliath's respective operating teams work well together.

Step 3. Goliath-customer decides it would be safer (and/or cheaper for Goliath) if they acquired supplier rather than buying Stuff from them.

Safer? Cheaper? I don't understand.

As Goliath-customer purchases more Stuff from David-supplier, the customer becomes increasingly dependent on supplier. The more unique or specialized the Stuff is, the more valuable it is, and the more vulnerable Goliath is.

The corollary is that David-supplier becomes increasingly reliant on Goliath-customer. Revenue concentration with Goliath means that losing this single account could put David out of business.

Mutual fragile (and increasingly uncomfortable) reliance.

Relieving that discomfort is why a garden-variety exit for startups is to an early or major customer.

Many Deal *"wheres"* and *"whens"*

Sparks may ignite from casual conversation between competitors, customers, or suppliers at a social event or an industry trade show. Or a pop-up restaurant. Or the sidelines of your daughter's soccer game. Or a basketball court.

Anywhere humans meet and talk. Suppliers usually have more than one impromptu, on-and-off talk with more than one customer, and customers with more than one supplier.

Many Deal *"hows"*

Neither life nor negotiations are linear. You can get from Point A to Point C without passing through Point B. (Think internet transmissions, connections, and modalities).

Seller (or Buyer) may say something direct or oblique.

David-companies (smaller, nimble, and entrepreneurial) function and communicate differently than Goliath-companies (larger, slower moving, and more institutional). That's not a criticism or endorsement of either style.

There is logic to why David functions like David, and valid reasons why Goliath functions like Goliath. Organizations operate and communicate (internally and externally) in a manner appropriate for their relative size and scale.

DealDances may be subtle. Glimmers appear early and are implicit in numerous counterparty interactions. The corporate courtship is replete with deal-suggestive banter, and what passes in business as corporate flirting.

In one such scenario an innovative tech startup David-company was negotiating the initial multi-year arrangement (Step 1) of what ultimately resulted in a sale to Goliath (Step 3). The startup's calculated high risk was dedicating most of their limited human resources trying to earn a long-term contract and relationship with a global company.

A flagship sale. (A flagship sail?)

David's two Institutional Advocates at Goliath (technology and marketing executives) were taking a high risk that David (and its fabulous non-commercialized technology) would develop quickly enough to perform a vital service for Goliath, giving them a differentiated marketplace advantage.

Months of contract negotiation with Goliath's lawyers were uniformly characterized as "great discussions" and "great meetings." That was "great." We were "grateful." But there was no signed agreement and no obvious time horizon.

To break the morass, to force a decision, David reluctantly delivered an ultimatum to Goliath.

Enter the exclusive long-term contract by Tuesday, or we'll disengage, "having no choice but to turn our resources to your competitors." (Recall consulting-speak's *forcing function*.)

On a heavily attended Thursday afternoon conference call five days before the looming deadline, we expressed skepticism about Goliath's corporate ability (not intention) to comply with the timetable.

Me (as Senior Strategic Advisor):	"You said you need a 'few' more headquarter approvals before signing. When I say 'a few' I mean two, three, or *maybe* four. What do *you* mean?"

Goliath Counterparty (after lengthy, *lengthy* silence):	"We just counted. Twenty-eight. Some in New York, London, and South America, and several in India."

The deal universe of *who*, *where*, and *when* had just exploded.

What did we hear and see? Goliath couldn't get all approvals on time. Not challenging. Unachievable.

Global Company's need and desire to enter into a multi-year, exclusive agreement with us was authentic. Economic and operational terms agreed to. Shared business motivation to close. The institutional advocates at Goliath were serious and competent, pushing to close, not stalling to gain negotiating leverage.

The common danger and enemy of the real counterparties-in-interest (the Advocate Duo and us) was Goliath's institutional policies and red-tape sludge. No specific individual was trying to sabotage a Closing.

CEO (to me about failed deal deadline):	"What should I do?"

Me: "Fly to Goliath's corporate headquarters where the Advocate Duo are. Stay with them until you do or don't have a deal. Your presence intensifies pressure on each of the twenty-eight individuals whose approval is needed.

"*Don't* ask permission to go. They might say no."

READER ASIDE: It's much easier to be the advice-*giver* (me) instead of advice-*taker* (CEO). Developing tactics is critical. Executing them is the whole ballgame.

Our CEO's body language was negative. He didn't want to intrude or make his presence seem like an overt threat.

I respected his perspective but (fortunately for the deal) didn't share it. This wasn't straightforward like the distressed Family business where all decision makers could be assembled in a single room for a single day. It still called out for a variation on the broad principle that **If it's important, do it in person.**

Me: "By being at the same location, you'll bond with Advocate Duo as joint victims of their bureaucracy.

"Right now, with you 'here' and them 'there,' it's *us*-David versus *them*-Goliath.

"If you and Advocate Duo are physically in the same place, your trio becomes *us*-David versus *them*-Goliath (the approving bureaucrats).

"Your collective visibility will make the Duo more powerful and effective internally with their colleagues, making it easier for them to accomplish your shared objective."

He flew to HQ where the newly formed Transaction Trio meta-phorically linked arms, aligned themselves against their common enemy, and closed Friday night, eight days later!

Even with our virtuoso tactical maneuvering, my inner cynic be-lieves Closing occurred only because everyone at headquarters wanted to get home for their weekends and get our CEO out of their offices!!!

> **READER ASIDE:** How was signing the multi-year Exclu-sive Contract the beginning of Goliath's subsequent acquisi-tion of David? Isn't this contract the *ending* of this deal?

Nope. The entire multi-year contract period becomes an M&A negotiation dance.

Viewed from a long-term acquisition perspective, the contract Closing was the invisible Big Bang for the later *informal* acquisi-tion. The virtually non-stop transactional process was largely conducted between Buyer and Seller within the confines of their customer-supplier contractual relationship.

During the contract period, each gets a sense of how their respective organizations function. The "Customer-Potential Buyer" experi-ences firsthand what might otherwise be deal diligence by observing how well supplier, its colleagues, and its technology performs.

Does the Stuff arrive on time? Does it work well? Does David un-derpromise and overdeliver or vice versa?

Customer-supplier relationships involve a mutual learning curve, bridging inherent organizational behavior and communication style differences. Both counterparties need to get what they need. When working together builds trust and personal relationships or-ganically, a larger deal is facilitated.

Every customer-supplier

- personal interaction,
- digital exchange, and
- casual conversation

is a step in the corporate "pas de deux" (a ballet dance for two) that may (may not) result in a later acquisition.

Every

- committee presentation from supplier to customer,
- vocabulary choice (think of words as billboards), and
- piece of sales promotional material

either *advances* selling the business (by creating positive feelings) or *impairs* an ultimate transaction (by sowing doubt and creating negative feelings).

CEOs who are long-term corporate strategists appropriately impose a view, a story, and tactics for each seemingly insignificant, non-deal interaction. It's all framing. It's all staging.

As the initial contract period expires, contractual renegotiation approaches, and Goliath can proceed several ways.

Goliath (posturing):	"We're not sure if we *can* extend the contract."
David (posturing in return):	"We're not sure we're *willing* to extend the *exclusive* contract."

Both politely (and lightly) outline the cost to the other counterparty if something positive doesn't happen. Point/Counterpoint. Pleasantries have been exchanged. Let the games begin.

The significance of all the pre-acquisition discussions ("foreshadowing" if this were a novel) occurring at an operating level begins to surface. They all trace back to the initial negotiation of the long-term contract.

Goliath can now make an indirect, oblique approach (see below). Goliath commits nothing by dangling verbal bait to see if David would bite.

Customer (as contract is going to either be extended or terminated):	"We have a great customer-supplier relationship. My people love working with your people. They share lots of common values. "I wonder if there's any way we could *expand* our relationship?"

Expand? What? Subtlety incarnate.

Of course, there's much to be said for a *direct* approach. The head of Goliath's corporate development team calls Supplier-CEO and asks, "Can we talk?" Not as funny as when Joan Rivers says it, but clearer.

Nothing mysterious. Corporate Development's function is doing deals. Trying to initiate a direct, straight-up discussion.

If this multi-year contract turns into an acquisition, it's fair to conclude either there was no Big Bang, *or* the Big Bang started with the multi-year contract negotiation and peaked in the Corporate Headquarter's Closing.

With that shared background, we knew Buyer's internal universe, players, and patterns. They knew us by name. We were comfortable we had a ticket to ride our way through their corporate thicket to a successful business sale. And we did.

Without that confidence, we would almost certainly have declined corporate development's invitation to "talk."

Some Deal "wheres"

Trade shows are trailer parks for strategic Buyers.

For active business buyers (or aspiring sellers), physical industry tradeshows or association meetings (not online digital meetings) are the equivalent of trailer parks for encyclopedia sellers: small places that are dense and customer target-rich.

Integrated business and social elements foster an unusual corporate and interpersonal environment and dynamics designed for corporate trolling.

This is what the panorama looks like.

Row after row of company booths are packed together. (How convenient!) In a normal business day eager corporate buyers can knock on dozens of deal doors, conversing with business owners (including those who aren't thinking of selling).

Serial buyers put the bait out again and again to see who takes it.

Unscripted, unplanned get togethers at a trade show or association meeting can be the first step in a long unfolding, dating/mating dance. Not groveling, but plainly pandering with unsolicited compliments. Encyclopedia redux.

Exploration is not commitment.

Not for buyer; not for seller. The exploration, however, can be more or less unmistakable or transparent.

Serial buyer (to competitor):	"If you're ever interested in selling, call me first. You run a great business and would be a wonderful partner."
National Retail Goliath (to David, with a sort-of-laugh like it's a joke):	"When you want to sell your business, I'm the obvious buyer. Let me know. I don't have stores in your region."
Regional Retail David (*chuckling*):	"I'll add you to the long list of people with the same question and give you the same answer. I'm having fun. Kicking butt. Zero interest in selling at any price."

Insignificant variations on this theme occurred, tradeshow after tradeshow. Smiles. Mutual laughter. Light and lively.

The break came in year five. National competitor delivered a more direct message, equal parts invitation and threat.

National Retail Goliath (to David):	"I've avoided retail locations near you out of respect for your business prowess and entrenched position. But I'm running out of new geographical territories to expand into. Soon I'll be working with tenant brokers to open stores in your area."
Regional Retail David:	"Information is appreciated, but I'm not worried. I have home field advantage. *You're* the visiting team. I've got all Class 'A' sites locked up. What's left are 'B' and 'C' sites. I'll clean your clock.
	"But *maybe* we should talk now before you make a costly mistake. At the right price (meaning the *right* price) maybe I could be persuaded to sell.
	"Maybe not.
	"Paying me a boatload would be more profitable for you than competing with me!"

Spirited negotiations followed, but Regional Retail David set the tone early for the highly favorable acquisition that closed months later.

He sang a great song replete with persuasive lyrics, chorus, and refrain. It was way too early to sing the Seller's Mantra expressing his need for Certainty and Confidentiality. Those words would have indicated he was more eager to entertain a discussion than he really was.

That multi-year interplay is an example of super-slow Big Bangs. The earliest interactions were so casual that neither counterparty may even remember them. They may have been reflexive conversations by each rather than intentional by either.

A few Deal *"whys"* and *"hows"*

Surface motivation for most sellers is straight-forward: *money*. Don't overthink this. Money may or may not be the root of all evil but it's unquestionably the root of most deals.

Non-economic factors may be equally important (even if less obvious) and should never be discounted or ignored.

Founder-as-fiduciary:	"My investors will get a 600% return. It gives me joy knowing their trust and faith in me was rewarded. Selling now may be selling 'too soon,' but I'll sleep very well for the rest of my life!"
CEO relief from management and operations:	"I'm tired and need to *retire*. There's no internal successor. I don't want to hire and trust an outsider to run my business. The only way to retire is to sell."
Personal Validation:	"My business was so important and successful that Global Giant bought it. The *Wall Street Journal* will write an article. I'll go from anonymous to famous; everyone will know my name and story. Lifetime bragging rights!"

Relief. Validation. Recognition. Some combination of the above, but in varying proportions.

There are almost as many motivations as there are people. How can we best use the realization that money is necessary but may not be sufficient?

If you're at a sticking point with a not-yet-willing seller, handing them an awesome press release may be more impactful (and cheaper) than increasing your offer by $10 million.

Buyer's *CEO* **to Seller:**	"I don't want to seem presumptuous. After our last session we all thought there was real momentum to completing this deal. So we took the liberty of preparing a draft press release to share with you announcing the acquisition. Here it is."
Buyer's *intermediary* **to Seller:**	"This is our CEO's quote: 'Mary Smith, Seller's Founder, is one of the most extraordinary business-people I've ever encountered. Visionary. Creative. Intrepid. A once-in-a-generation talent. She built a company we're truly honored and humbled to add to our corporate family.'"
Buyer CEO to Seller:	"There aren't adequate words to express our admiration for your accomplishments. What you've launched is one of the great innovation success stories of the twenty-first century. The equal of Steve Jobs and Apple. We're eager to share your story with the world."

Hand the press release to Seller. Hard copy, not digital. Tangible. Palpable. Invoke the powerful sense of touch.

Spell out the entire value proposition (benefits to Seller) through (what you imagine to be) their eyes. They aren't you. What motivates you doesn't necessarily motivate them. You're not negotiating with a mirror image.

How do you convert a now *willing* seller into a *motivated* seller? By letting a vacillating Seller who isn't yet emotionally committed to selling her company feel the consequences. Stir deep emotions. Appeal to ego. Make the personal and financial consequences real and desirable and tangible. Those motivators propel deals to close.

Question: How do you make them feel and hear *today* the lucrative end results they'll enjoy and feel emotionally *tomorrow* if they sell their business?

Answer: *People absorb information and experience emotion more easily going from concrete to abstract than abstract to concrete.*

Let's revisit some door-to-door lessons.

More than once the decisive moment came when a prospective customer was handed an encyclopedia volume. They held it, handed it to their spouse, turned pages to beautiful illustrations, and looked up a subject that gave them joy.

All those actions (not just thoughts) emotionally converted the books from mine to theirs, even if only for a moment. They helped them experience the future pleasure they would receive after making the purchase. *Gain.*

When they gave it back to me? *Loss.*

That same persuasive selling sequence (creating a wonderful feeling of gain, followed by a painful feeling of loss), applies to encyclopedia sales, in-store retail sales, and negotiating corporate acquisition deals.

Don't pick up a puppy in a pet store unless you want to own a dog

Selling encyclopedias, houses, pets, or businesses involves the same elements of possession, gain, and loss even if they have different names and occur in different settings.

Were you ever in a pet store? Did the salesperson *let* your child hold a puppy? (Great salespeople *insist* you do so). As soon as someone holds a puppy it becomes "theirs" emotionally.

Customers cuddle and pet the dog-in-training which looks at them adoringly with large, liquid eyes.

Your child's face lights up and they bounce up and down with excitement. If someone (images of mean parents spring to mind) doesn't buy *"their puppy"* for them, children perceive loss even though they never owned the puppy.

We all do. *You* don't like loss. *I* don't like loss. It hurts.

Because of that, oodles of parents buy oodles of poodles (however reluctantly), and the puppy deal closes.

Possession is 9/10 of any sale.

Conceptually, it's all the same.

Persuading a seller whose company is not "on the market" to engage and sell their business is invoking as many of the prospective seller's senses and heart-felt emotions as a pet store owner selling a puppy.

You want the seller to figuratively *taste* the money, *feel* the money, and react as if they are *holding* the money and *spending* it. You want them to leaf through travel brochures to decide where they'll go, and what they'll do with their newfound life, freed from constraints of time and money.

How do you trigger comparable emotions (endorphin rush) by having a *future* business seller cognitively "hold a puppy"? What alchemy catalyzes an off-the-market seller into a willing seller, and finally to a motivated seller?

Substitute cash for puppy and you're well on your way.

People understand intangible "stuff" more easily if you start with concrete/specific "stuff." You'll get agreement more quickly by saying "I'll pay you $100 million for your business," instead of saying "I'll pay you a lot of money."

Who knows what your counterparty thinks a "lot of money" means? If they think "a lot" means $500 million then your $100 million offer sounds pitifully small. You've created your own barrier to making a sale.

Without context, it's difficult to translate *your* words into *their* reality. One hundred million dollars sounds like a lot of money, but it may not be tangible enough to motivate a seller to sell. (How much different does *$100* million sound as a cluster of words than *$200* million?)

How can you make that amount of cash real? Break it down into smaller increments that are relatable in daily human terms.

> **Buyer:** "Don't think of this as a *deal*. Think of it as a *golden parachute* with a fully funded retirement plan! After taxes, you can spend $1 million *every week* forever and never run out of money."

How much happiness will the money buy? What would Seller like it to buy?

> **Buyer:** "I can picture the rest of your life. You lying on the beach. Fishing in your boat. Drinking ice-cold beer. I'll bet your golf handicap goes down six strokes. I'm jealous but happy for you."

The more successfully you assist Seller into feeling emotionally joyful, the more easily you'll make the deal. Sing, paint, and reinforce images about Seller's life as if they already sold the business and received the cash.

After Closing they'll have money and freedom to enjoy their lives, families, and hobbies instead of people and operations to manage and economic risk to bear.

Pull that happiness forward. Make it tangible and concrete right now. This minute. "Say it with me. It's a great trade."

The certainty and comfort Seller didn't even know they wanted starts to sound awfully attractive. How kind of Buyer to have provided it!

It's time to tiptoe through other transactional tulips.

Chapter 6 Key Takeaways

- Whatever industry you're in, everyone's in the relationship and information business.

You don't know *when* you'll want to sell (or *when* someone wants to buy) your company, but you generally know *who* the most likely suspects are.

It's good *business*, important *information*, and prudent *exit planning* to be familiar with the universe of probable buyers. Build strong personal connections with your *natural acquirors* (customers, suppliers, competitors).

Learn who you do (or don't) like, and whose words you do (or don't) believe long before you engage in a possible M&A discussion.

Cash is fungible. Trust isn't.

- The most important counterparty for Seller to know and trust may be counterintuitive; it's *Seller*. What's really motivating you to sell or consider selling? Fear? Greed? Ego?

You have to be rigorously honest. Know the enemy and try not to make it yourself. Don't make Buyer's job easy.

- *Don't* count your money.

- *Don't* dream about the Bahamas.

- *Don't* operate and act as if it's a done deal until about a week *after* Closing.

All those quintessentially human reactions strengthen Buyer's leverage and weaken yours.

WHEN PEOPLE ARE PAYING TULIP BULB PRICES, AND YOU OWN TULIP BULBS, YOU SHOULD SELL THEM

At the beginning of a technology "revolution," I was a stockholder and Director of a venture-funded company (Tennessee Technologies). We were an industry pioneer in the right place at the right time. Prospects for growth appeared unlimited.

As frequently happens in financial gold rushes, numerous competitors (Goliaths as well as Davids) were anxious to combine with others and achieve relevance. The sector was hungry for size, scale, and market share, eager for consolidation. There were going to be big corporate winners and losers. Investment and buyout money was plentiful.

Adam Smith's eighteenth-century rules about supply and demand remain valid. In *Wealth of Nations* he posited that if supply of a product remains constant, and demand increases, the "invisible hand" of the marketplace will guide the price higher until supply and demand are in equilibrium.

Demand for our type of company was incredibly high. *Supply* was incredibly limited. The result was inevitable.

Deal prices were soaring to unprecedented levels compared to traditional valuation metrics. If the average transaction purchase price for a Tennessee Technologies-type business was historically 4-6 times a company's annual revenues for the prior year, now it was 20-25 times *next year's* revenues.

If there was a limit, it seemed no closer than the sky.

Our unbridled enthusiasm was modestly bridled by remembering a cautionary story from seventeenth-century Netherlands. Brightly colored tulips briefly became the worldwide status symbol for fashionable gardens and their owners. A full-fledged mass mania to own tulip bulbs swept the globe.

Demand for contracts to purchase tulip bulbs overwhelmed supply. Prices rose swiftly from one Dutch guilder per tulip bulb in 1634 to 60 guilders three years later, more than ten times the annual income of a skilled craft worker.

At that point a default on a tulip bulb purchase contract panicked the market. Everyone tried to sell their contracts simultaneously. *Supply* (i.e., tulip bulb contracts available for sale) soared. *Demand* plummeted. The price crashed by ~98% in only a few days. Fortunes were lost.

Despite our apparently shimmering future we knew no market goes up forever. Whether we should sell the company before an inevitable price crash came was raised at every monthly Director's meeting.

Veteran Wall Streeters on the board had an annoying habit of constantly invoking the following bromide from the financial world:

> Bulls make money.

> Bears make money.

> Pigs get slaughtered.

Was Tennessee Technologies a twenty-first century corporate tulip bulb? Where was our company on the scale of one to sixty guilders? 10? 58? 72?

Didn't want to sell too soon and didn't want to sell too late.

Question (from earnest, aspiring Dealjammer): How do you *know* the right time?

Answer: You *don't*. You *can't*. (I was bummed to learn this too.)

Decision-making would be so easy if any of us ever definitively knew whether they were being a bull, bear, pig, or tulip bulb-owner. But we don't.

Analyze your choices as dispassionately as possible. Then with conviction (as if you definitively knew you were right) execute your decision perfectly.

As Seller your ideal circumstances are that a financially capable, motivated, and competent Buyer emerges on your doorstep seeking to buy you without being invited to do so.

This starting point for engagement makes it clear you weren't actively trying sell your business. If you weren't, it's more likely than not that you're not a motivated seller. Someone's trying to buy you, but you weren't trying to be sold.

Question: Why was this significant distinction so clear in Paul's Parts?

Answer: The CEO-owner who thought our CEO was a Messenger from God took *none* of the conventional actions a company actively trying to sell itself would have taken. He had *not*:

- hired an investment banker,
- initiated contact with potential buyers,
- set up a data room so buyers could easily conduct their due diligence, or
- spent days talking through all the scenarios, tax implications, and pitfalls with his legal and accounting professionals.

Before his religious summons came (and we serendipitously appeared on his doorstep), Paul was simply running his company. Business-as-normal.

What made Paul's negotiating posture so strong? He was seemingly unconcerned whether he sold his business or not. Charley's Consolidated wanted to *buy* the business much more than Paul's Parts' CEO wanted to *sell* it.

He had the business, and numbers favored him. There was only one Paul's Parts. There were only two days in which Paul's Parts was available to be bought, not sold.

In a perfect world, every seller would like to be Paul's Parts (or at least give the appearance of being Paul's Parts). Sellers tend to receive the maximum price if they're *bought* rather than *sold*.

Wait. There's a difference?

When a buyer takes the first step in an acquisition by reaching out, some negotiating leverage invariably favors Seller. If Seller truly wasn't even remotely contemplating selling, then Seller has even more leverage.

While a company that's approached first may be a *willing* seller at a remarkably favorable price, they're unlikely to be a *motivated* seller. They don't *have* to sell. They don't *need* to sell. Their indifference about selling (or not selling) is their leverage.

Even though it's not yet a perfect world, a public company (Goliath strategic buyer) approached Tennessee Technologies inquiring vaguely whether they could "chat" with us.

A quick review of their SEC filings revealed they'd made five acquisitions but no strategic investments. We were confident their real inquiry was whether Tennessee was (or could be persuaded to be) for sale, not whether they could invest *in* our company.

We prepared for the requested conference call based on that assumption. After superficial chitchat, Buyer's CEO almost immediately dropped any pretense, stopped social niceties, and bluntly asked what purchase price it would take for them to buy us.

Needless to say, this is *not* recommended strategy.

Our CEO (the majority owner) was an extremely experienced negotiator. His conversation-ending-response was flawless.

CEO-majority owner (with a twinkle in his eyes, face, and voice): "Well, selling *now* really isn't in our five-year plan. We're looking to grow organically or to buy other businesses.

"This must be silly season. Every week investment bankers or one of your competitors are calling unsuccessfully trying to throw money at us.

"There really isn't any reason to engage with you unless you'd like *us* to buy *you*! Thanks so much for calling, and good luck with your efforts."

Is there any way the CEO could have more clearly said "No, we aren't for sale"?

Really?

His sparse words were pitch perfect. His tone of voice was casual. There wasn't a hint of tension or interest in it. His cadence was slow and unstudied. Nothing conveyed that he was even remotely motivated by Buyer's outreach.

Flawless delivery. He instantly communicated,

- how *self-sufficient* ("lots of cash") and *valuable* Tennessee Technologies was (people are offering ridiculous amounts of money),

- how *much* competition Buyer would have if they wanted to buy the company, and

- *where* the competition would come from ("your competitors"). Goliath wasn't the only uninvited company ("investment bankers and your competitors") calling to initiate an investment or an acquisition.

In fewer than seventy-five words the CEO's speech may not have matched Lincoln's Gettysburg Address for substance and brevity, but in sports vernacular, "it deserves to be in the conversation."

The business translation was that he wasn't a *motivated* seller nor even a *willing* seller. Classic reverse psychology.

Not to our surprise (and I hope not yours) the spurned buyer called back a week later.

Emboldened by the success of our first assumption, we made another aggressive inference, i.e., in the interim between phone calls Buyer was testing other M&A waters. Were any fish in a limited pond of sellers hungry enough to take their bait?

Our theory was Buyer called other companies and discovered:

- they weren't for sale (making us *scarcer*), or
- weren't as desirable an acquisition as we were (making us *massively* scarcer).

Their market check further confirmed our rarity, increasing our negotiating leverage and perceived value.

> **Buyer:**   "You have a great management team. You're admirably positioned for long-term growth.
>
> "We heard you last week that you aren't *actively* pursuing a sale, but we'd still like to visit and chat. It won't be a waste of your time. We're a very serious buyer."

Despite our studied words of indifference, we weren't trying to fool ourselves. Never believe your own selling pitch. As physicist Richard Feynman observed, "The first principle is that you must not fool yourself and you are the easiest person to fool."

In reality, we were passively open to *being acquired* but not actively trying to be sold. They were trying to buy us. With sufficient economic motivation even the most unmotivated of sellers may become willing to discuss the prospect of selling.

What could exploring hurt? (We'll consider that in some depth in the next chapter.) We'd never have better negotiating leverage in a transaction.

We decided to sell our corporate tulip bulbs *if* (but only if) we could get a tulip bulb price.

Our scarcity was real and market-validated. Tennessee Technologies was an accidental (but grateful) beneficiary. We didn't have to artificially create scarcity by limiting free encyclopedias to one couple per neighborhood.

A tulip-bulb price ($196 million) was agreed to; 25 times next year's annual revenues. The tippy-top (tulip-top?) of manic pricing and a feeding frenzy.

At our insistence, eventually all DealCirclers met in person to resolve and finalize remaining issues by going on a line-by-line basis through Buyer's massive proposed acquisition agreement.

When clients are in the room with their lawyers, the principals' presence puts a "brake" on lawyer behavior, tends to lower negotiating temperature, and limits overly aggressive attorney advocacy as well as posturing.

People will say things more stridently and harshly in an email than they would ever say on a phone. People will say things more stridently and harshly on a phone call than they would ever say in person. *(Propinquity counts.)*

Knowing you have to look someone in the eye and continue interacting with them for hours tends to eliminate some unpleasant and belligerent behavior.

Is that all?

No. Unlike their lawyers, principals have incentive and authority to either accept a counterparty's position or reach compromises on an issue. It's the principals' money.

Their lawyers can't. It's *not* their money.

Despite that (or perhaps because of that) lengthy, impassioned debates can arise between lawyers regarding a miniscule deal provision.

How should an item be resolved as a matter of *principle*. That's an appropriate courtroom approach where objective resolutions are decided by an impartial judge or jury.

Maybe not so appropriate in a subjective, one-on-one, partisan negotiation. There's no legal right or wrong; there's only persuasion and belief.

The verbal skirmish below occurred as the counterparty's attorneys tried to reach agreement on a conceptual, principled basis about a disputed financial provision.

> **NOTE TO READER:** Decide whether you want to laugh or cry if this exchange is irritatingly familiar to you.

> **Lawyer #1:** "The Supreme Court's decision in *Smith v. Jones* clearly held that acquisition costs like this transfer tax are Seller's responsibility because they 'run with the property.'"

> **Lawyer #2:** "*No!* There's an important exception in footnote seventeen that clearly applies."

> **Lawyer #1:** "The *Smith* decision issue is *exactly* like Section 3(A)(iii)(*a*) of *this* Acquisition Agreement and should be resolved the same way."

> **Lawyer #2:** "This isn'*t remotely* like Section 3.
>
> "Even if that section were relevant, the accurate cross-reference would be to 3(A)(iii) (*b*). This is completely different."

Seller's CEO listened patiently as this display of arcane legal warriorship went on and on. Finally, with a totally guileless expression on his face, he said:

> **Seller CEO:** "It's really fabulous to hear the two of you exchange such educated views on this topic. I'm a pretty simple guy. Can you *monetize* the issue? How much are we talking about in dollars and cents?"

In the *abstract*, this provision could be a toss-up going in favor of buyer or seller. It became *non-abstract* as soon as our CEO forced it to be explicit. The lawyers quickly agreed the amount in dispute was $50,000.

Our CEO asked the best question without agreeing or disagreeing with either esteemed lawyer. Focus on the concrete issue and the desired outcome. Math is neither emotional nor conceptual.

Many issues are most easily resolved by monetizing them.

There's a valid line of thinking that negotiators should never split the difference. Like all sound guidelines (including my maxims) there are limits, exceptions, and context. You can't let literal words of a rule obscure its broad purpose or utility.

> **Seller CEO** "You know what? This $50,000 issue isn't
> **(to Buyer CEO):** worth our respective time or trouble. Let's
> just split the difference. We'll pay $25,000
> and you pay $25,000. Doesn't that seem
> fair? Then we can move on to the next issue."

In a transaction of this size, the amount in contention didn't rise to the level of a rounding error for Buyer or Seller. Neither should have felt compelled economically to "win" an issue whose financial consequences were so small.

Our CEO pushed for a quick resolution of a financially unimportant matter that was unnecessarily creating negotiating gridlock and decreasing deal momentum.

Why?

FIRST RULE OF DEAL DYNAMICS: *A deal in motion tends to stay in motion; a deal at rest tends to die.*

For reasons unknown, Buyer didn't accept Seller's suggestion.

Since there wasn't a quick acceptance, our CEO said:

> **Seller CEO:** "You know what. This issue is clearly important to you. Let's resolve it *your* way.
> We'll pay the *entire* $50,000."

It's easy (and tactically valuable) to be gracious about inconsequential matters. Build goodwill for your cooperation. Especially easy if your net proceeds only decrease from $196 million to $195,950,000!

Later on (when a disagreement involved $1 million) our CEO asserted with considerable force (and a straight face),

> **Seller CEO:** "Well, we resolved the last economic issue (the transfer tax) in your favor. So this one should go to us."

Talk about false equivalence! Arguably "fair." Buyer won one issue so Seller should win one issue. Economically "silly" when one issue is $50,000 (less than a rounding error) and the other is $1 million (*much* more than a rounding error).

We deducted $50,000 from the purchase price and accepted $195,950,000 total;

- $193,950,000 paid in cash at Closing, and
- $2 million cash in a two-year escrow account.

There was no personal indemnification liability to any selling stockholders. The only post-Closing financial exposure of the stockholders was whether we would receive all, none, or only a portion of the escrow amount. That money served as Buyer's sole recourse for breach of transactional reps and warranties.

When we evaluated whether the purchase price was acceptable, I assumed (as I usually do) we would never receive any of the escrowed amount.

Not that we weren't entitled to the money or had done anything bad. Unhappy prior experiences caused me to proceed with extreme caution and assume Buyer would do something untoward.

Even if we received *nothing* from the $2 million cash placed in the escrow account, we would all still consider it a good deal that we would collectively want to enter into.

Said differently, would we have accepted an offer for $194 million cash at Closing with no future money in escrow? Absolutely yes. In a New York minute.

There's a subset of buyer's remorse (an *aftermath*), that (now and again) emerges post-Closing. Time passes. The purchase that seemed *irresistible* then now seems *very* resistible. Just because the deal has closed doesn't meant it's closed and set in stone.

Some folks negotiate a deal first and then sign the contract. Others sign a contract first and then negotiate the deal. Think about it.

Months and months after the deal closed, Buyer was angry (and embarrassed). With the illuminating benefit of hindsight, they belatedly concluded that in the buying frenzy for a rapidly consolidating young industry they badly overpaid and severely "under-diligenced."

The sky-high, gold-rush prices paid had receded (as they inevitably do). Buyer's negotiators (their CEO and General Counsel) clearly felt foolish and/or stupid. How could they explain and justify to their Directors and stockholders why they had paid triple what the business was worth only two years later?

Given a choice, few humans choose to conclude that they are stupid, mendacious, or incompetent. If *they* weren't stupid, mendacious or incompetent, then by the process of elimination it had to be that *we* were.

Like most escrow agreements, Buyer was obligated to promptly notify Seller about any alleged claims for violations of Seller's reps and warranties as they arose (or were discovered). That mechanism gives Seller the chance to investigate (or protest) a claim while facts are fresh.

Buyer waited until the last possible day (i.e., one year plus 364 days after Closing) before raising a motley collection of non-fact-based claims.

To state the obvious, it's impossible (*not improbable*) that claims aggregating the full escrow amount arose the day before the escrow should have been released.

Bad faith at its baddest.

All counterparties had agreed that escrow disputes would be referred to *non*-binding mediation (mutually trying to avoid the cost and expense of litigation). Buyer invoked the process.

At the end of a marathon, eleven-hour dispute-resolution session (Buyer in a fourth floor room, Seller in a fifth floor room, and mediators shuttling between us), a mediator pulled me privately into a hallway:

> **Mediator:**   "You know, sometimes the hardest position
> to be in a litigation or mediation is when
> you're 100% correct and totally blameless.
> That's all I'm saying."

I couldn't have been more confused. What was he trying to tell me?

His observation was emotionally insightful, obliquely communicating the mediators' conclusion that Sellers were blameless. No violations of reps and warranties. No facts supporting Buyer's claims. As soon as that was communicated to Buyer, the nonbinding mediation process would be over.

Odds were good Buyer wouldn't accept this evaluation. They'd sue us rather than release our funds. These were seriously embarrassed, ego-bruised executives. Our $2 million would remain in escrow while a costly litigation process ensued.

They'd be spending corporate time and dollars litigating. We'd be spending our time and our dollars litigating. ***You can only spend one dollar one time. And you can only spend one hour one time.***

I had repeatedly communicated that it was incomprehensible that anyone would expect me/us to give up money when we'd done nothing wrong. Moral righteousness on full display. (Not usually helpful.)

The mediator's comments hit home, and prompted an important (but unpleasant) flashback. Another unlearned-lesson.

When I was CEO and Managing Partner of a law firm, we had a fee dispute with a new client who had retained us because they were about to be venture-funded. As part of our normal intake procedures, we reviewed the client's personal history with him. In his words, after making a fortune he dedicated his life to others, adopting and educating numerous orphans. A saint-like human.

As part of the Fund's more rigorous pre-Closing diligence procedures, their litigation search revealed dozens of legal judgments against our client. Super *un*saintlike. With total justification the Fund didn't close their investment.

I had been directly deceived and actively bamboozled.

We sent the client our invoice for legal services rendered. After months of non-payment, lies, and evasion, we finally sued him. (Only time I've ever sued anyone.)

Moments before trial the judge took me into a courthouse conference room and inquired sympathetically about the case's background. Then she came directly to the heart of the matter.

> **Judge:**   "Mr. CEO and Managing Partner. Juries don't like liars; but they *hate* lawyers. Settle the case."

In the *abstract* I'd rather be "right" than "wrong." In the *concrete* neither is necessarily decisive. Many disputes get resolved because it costs less to compromise (or even to completely cave) and pay unearned money rather than pay even more in time, ongoing anger, and legal fees to prove you were right.

Pyrrhic victories are overrated.

We took the judge's "suggestion" and settled my law firm's lawsuit for a fraction of what we were owed. (Not that I'm bitter.)

The same dollar-based analytical prism caused us to settle the Tennessee Technologies mediation, releasing $1 million from escrow to Buyer we clearly didn't owe so we could get the other $1 million. (Not that I'm bitter.)

My takeaway?

Don't get confused. When a counterparty says, "It's not about the money, it's the principle," it's not true.

You may *think* it's not the money. Your counterparty may even *believe* it's not the money. Rest assured. It's not the money; *it's the money.*

In deciding to sell Tennessee Technologies, our analysis assumed we'd potentially get nothing from escrow. Our worst result would be receiving only $19**4** million. We'd have the chance to receive up to $19**6** million. (In actuality, we got $19**5** million.)

That's the level of outcome certainty sellers should strive for, and we'll explore further in the next chapter.

Chapter 7 Key Takeaways

- *People (not spreadsheets) are the epicenter of every deal.*

The marketplace for buying and selling private companies is an illiquid, fragmented bazaar. Businesses are "worth" only the price a specific ready, willing, and able buyer pays.

Irrational exuberance is real. Markets go *up*. (Hip, hip, hooray!) Markets go *down*. (Boo!)

When people are paying tulip-bulb prices, and you own tulip bulbs, you should sell them. Get the cash before the crash.

- If you *do* have self-discipline, then *"Exploration is not commitment."* You have the power to stop negotiating and say "no." If you *don't*, don't start.

- Sellers appropriately value certainty. Don't esteem it so highly that searching for it paralyzes you into inaction. If it does, the only price you can ever sell at is "more" and the only time you can ever do that is "later."

What *is* certain is you'll never know for sure if you're selling at the right time, to the right buyer, for the right amount. It's not *unknown*. It's *unknowable*.

- When issues can be resolved conceptually, do it. When they can't, *monetize* them.

How far apart are you and your counterparty concretely, in absolute dollars? Say it with me now. "It's not the money. It's the money."

CHAPTER 8

THE SELLER'S MANTRA IS CERTAINTY AND CONFIDENTIALITY

In religious contexts, a mantra is a word or sound repeated unceasingly to deeply immerse practitioners during their meditation (not their mediation).

The musical equivalent is a drone, a prolonged, deep, reverberating note (or tone cluster). Almost hypnotic. A technique used by Delta blues guitarists, sitar players, and bagpipers.

The melody changes while the drone sound maintains again and again and again. (Think, introduction to the Rolling Stones' "Paint it Black.")

The transactional equivalent is the *"Seller's Mantra"*; the Deal-Drone that should be repeated by every Seller to every Buyer over and over and over again from "NegotiationDayOne" to "NegotiationDaySign."

Seller to Buyer: "What I need is:

- *Certainty*, and
- *Confidentiality.*

"If our discussions leak and a deal doesn't close, my business and I will be damaged. That risk is real. That risk is costly. At the first *whisper* of a leak, regardless of source, I'll stop negotiating."

Seller's concern is on-target. The minimum goal should reflect the medical profession's Hippocratic oath that the first principle is to do no harm.

The process of selling a business epitomizes uncertainty. The Big Bang firecracker frequently fizzles. So the hungered-for bedrock element of *certainty* for Seller is confessional-quality-sanctity *confidentiality* during negotiations, and double that afterwards if the deal isn't concluded.

The Big Bad Bank-induced informal auction of financially distressed Impala showed us some high level costs to Seller of confidentiality lost and certainty lacked. Let's take a look at a *low* level; on the ground instead of 40,000 feet.

Even in the polar opposite of Impala (a single buyer in an informal, one-on-one private sale) confidentiality is hard to maintain.

People and paper produce problems

In the negotiation process, sophisticated sellers involve only individuals inside and outside their organization with a compelling need-to-know. Who? When? How long?

Seller's Negotiating Need	Supporting Cast
Historical financial information to provide Buyer.	Enter Seller's *CFO*.
Tax and accounting guidance.	Enter Seller's *lawyer* and *CPA*.
Sales pipeline prospects supporting financial projections given to Buyer.	Enter Seller's *EVP* of Marketing.
Communicate with Buyer.	Emails, texts, documents.

Seller's CFO, Lawyers, Accountants, and EVP have partners, spouses, and best friends. ("I *know* they can keep a secret.")

The longer the process, the larger Buyer's and Seller's respective DealCircle, the more certain it is that confidentiality will be breached, even in a well-conceived, non-auction transaction.

Odds are good the breach is unintentional. Odds are better it occurs.

That's *bad* news.

The *worse* news is that with a formal investment-banker-led process, no matter who runs it, Sellers should assume confidentiality will be breached. Hugely larger DealCircle.

People pilfer your personnel and customers.

Let's revisit Impala's informal auction. News of the sale forced by the Big Bad Bank was widely known in the industry, partly due to extensive industry bidder outreach, and partly due to nervous, overly chatty Impala Family members at their country clubs.

Not to mention suppliers and customers.

(Those of you with unshakeable conviction about the goodness of humanity may want to skip the next few pages.)

From marketplace reactions Buyer (Acquisitions R Us) inferred that the split-second rumors/news got out, Impala's *competitors* reached out to its customers with conversations like this:

> **#1:** "Why would you keep dealing with Impala? They're being sold? Isn't that a big risk for you?"

> **#2:** "Their bank pulled their loan and is forcing them to sell the business. Big time cash flow and product problems."

> **#3:** "Aren't you nervous about what will happen to their pricing policies and service capabilities?"

| **All Competitors:** | "Maybe you should switch your business to me now while it's a good time to do so. Protect yourself." |

What damaging questions were Impala's *customers* quite reasonably asking themselves?

| **Customer #1:** | "A major reason I buy from Seller is family ownership. Even after the warranty period expires they accept returns to protect the Family reputation. Easy to do business with. Prospective buyers are notoriously bad about honoring even timely warranties. They fight and deny everything. I'm worried." |

| **All customers:** | "Can I even *afford* to keep buying from Seller? Doesn't legitimate self-interest mean I should switch to another manufacturer before it's too late?" |

Impala's competitors were also trying to raid sales personnel and hire away productive employees. What siren song did they sing?

| **Competitors #1, 2, *and* 3:** | "Come work for me. We're stable and solid; not like your current boss. You know who you'll be working for." |

| **All Competitors:** | "Think about yourself, your family, and your future. You don't owe *their* Family anything. It's a tough world. Look out for yourself." |

As soon as marketplaces even *sense* a possible transaction, significant leverage switches to Buyer. Seller is weakened, under attack, and vulnerable.

If a deal doesn't close, the current (as well as future) value of Seller's business deteriorates simply as a result of breached confidentiality.

Whether intentional (competitors) or careless/inadvertent (everyone else), Seller is now damaged goods.

Those circumstances may transform even an unmotivated (previously unwilling) Seller who engaged in negotiations "out of *curiosity*" into a forced Seller out of *necessity*.

Advantage? Buyer.

Murphy's law isn't deal-specific but still applies

Never underestimate the universe's randomness or the power of Murphy's Law. "Whatever can go wrong will go wrong."

Our ownership group was selling a landmark downtown office building. The probable buyer accidentally forwarded their internal transaction analysis to us (including the top price they'd pay and why).

The subject line simply referenced the building's name. Nothing suggested our group wasn't the intended recipient. We all read the email with amazement.

Within fifteen minutes, an email arrived from Buyer marked "urgent" in the subject line, requesting us to delete the prior email without reading it.

If we hadn't already read the errant correspondence, we would have complied. But this genie was already out of this bottle. We couldn't not know what we already knew.

Remaining negotiations strongly favored us since we knew (to the penny) Buyer's purchasing limits and analysis.

There's no surprise ending to this story. We got the top price. It exceeded our intended ask. If we didn't, you should probably stop reading right now!

Successful Seller's Certainty Cornerstone

Of equal importance to confidentiality is *certainty*: certainty about every element in the deal *process* which leads to deal *outcome*. It's a remarkably long list for Seller to worry about.

Below are some legitimate concerns about *process* certainty.

Seller to Buyer: "How can I be *certain* you have:

- cash,

- knowledge,

- decision-making authority, and

- skill

to close the deal if we reach agreement?"

"How can I be *certain*:

- your lawyers won't run amuck in the definitive documents, effectively changing the economics of our Letter of Intent,

- you don't need anyone else's approval (inside or outside your company) to close, and

- you'll pay any post-Closing purchase price owed to me without trying to re-negotiate?"

Each additional Buyer approval needed (internal or external), each additional condition precedent to Closing, increases time, execution risk, and uncertainty to Seller.

Structural certainty.

In our earlier Legal Detour we talked about how deal structure (stock versus assets) impacts structural certainty for the counterparties. Sellers generally want to sell stock. Buyers want to buy assets. More detail would bog us down in the minutiae we mutually agreed to avoid.

High level? As Seller I want to be fully protected from liabilities to Buyer (and anyone else) after we close and I've sold my company.

Outcome certainty.

As Seller I want to know:

- *who* is paying me,
- *when* I'll get paid,
- *what* could impair/prevent that, and
- *when* I can fully exhale and breathe deeply because the deal and its consequences are irrevocably over.

That's structural *and* outcome certainty for Seller. All the money they received is really theirs. No one has a future claim against it.

Whether buyer or seller, I approach every negotiation thinking through the prism of the "Seller's Mantra."

At the same time 360-degree symmetry requires fully appreciating the *"Buyer's* Mantra." How can Buyer be sure that:

- Seller isn't using Buyer as a stalking horse to attract other higher bids, and
- the acquired business is what it appears to be, and worth what Buyer's paying?

Buyer's need for confidentiality and certainty is a fun house mirror of Seller's.

From Buyer's viewpoint, here's a sampling of bad things that can happen if confidentiality isn't maintained:

- Key Seller personnel and customers go to competitors, decreasing the business's value, or
- Competitors approach Seller to try to buy the company because they know it's "in play."

If the deal *doesn't* close and there are leaks in the market, the larger deal world may conclude:

- Buyer isn't competent,
- Buyer *is* competent but discovered bad facts about Seller so Buyer didn't want to close, or
- Seller walked because of bad Buyer behavior. That makes it

harder for Buyer to do their next transaction. They've lost trust and credibility in the deal marketplace.

Does that mean you should never do, or try to do, a deal? Of course not.

The world generally (and the deal world in particular) is inundated with uncertainty and risk. The Seller's Mantra exists despite the reality that absolute certainty can never be achieved, nor risk entirely eliminated.

Anyone who can't live with that inherent ambiguity should never do a deal, or try to do a deal. More to the point, they won't be *able* to do a deal. They'll experience too much emotional and intellectual dissonance.

The real-world solution is to accept only the level of risk and reward that lets you sleep at night, acknowledging that your analysis is never likely to be 100% correct. Murphy's Law can't be repealed.

Voltaire expressed this remarkably well: "Uncertainty is an uncomfortable position, but certainty is an absurd one."

Regrettably, enlightenment through education has eluded us yet again. Let's turn to a specific corporate caper, which torturously and slowly unfolded over the course of a year.

Chapter 8 Key Takeaways

The Seller's Mantra is Certainty and Confidentiality.

CONFIDENTIALITY The indispensable foundation for certainty is *confidentiality:* a state-of-being harder to obtain than people anticipate. If secrecy is violated, sellers lose more than buyers.

Buyers routinely volunteer confidentiality in a conversation. "Everything will remain just between the two of us." Perfect! Unless you believe movie titan Sam Goldwyn's sage observation that "a verbal contract isn't worth the paper it's printed on."

Sign a Confidentiality and Non-disclosure Agreement (NDA). Get agreed procedures to protect deal privacy and prevent transactional piracy.

At a *minimum* buyers and sellers should agree to:

- maintain segregated computer files with *zero trust* cyber-security protection for any documents or data exchanged,

- share information only on a *need-to-know-basis* with all Deal Circlers (internal as well as external), and

- use anonymous or *code names* in all documents and diligence materials.

CERTAINTY Repeat after me: "Smart sellers want *process, structural,* and *outcome* certainty."

As Seller, your negotiating leverage peaks the instant before the Letter of Intent is signed. After that it's all downhill.

A *thorough* LOI is more important than a *speedy* LOI. Seller should negotiate every possible major and minor economic provision, conditions to Closing, and Seller financial exposure post-Closing. Act in haste. Pay a heavy price at leisure.

STARTUPS ARE TIME, CASH, AND EMOTION VAMPIRES

Our early stage manufacturing company (Up-and-Comer) had breakthrough technology, validated in the lab but not yet commercialized, let alone scaled.

The product was so promising that we entered into an exclusive global distribution agreement with one of the world's largest and best-respected technology companies. A world-class brand name. A Goliath's Goliath.

They would sell our product to their enormous embedded customer base through their sales channel. After four painful years of development, we thought this relationship made us golden. But relatively soon, following many non-productive meetings, there was no way to fool ourselves.

This was a classic mismatch of styles, speeds, and needs. After a year there were absolutely no sales of any significance.

Anyone who has ever made (or frustratingly tried to make) an evangelical, business-to-business (B2B) sale knows no matter how conservative you think your financial projections are, initial product sales take *years* longer than you'd ever anticipate.

People *hate* change. People don't like taking risks. "Let's keep doing what we've done before."

In *The Prince*, Machiavelli framed it perfectly:

> *There is nothing more difficult to take in hand, more perilous to conduct, or more uncertain in its success, than to take the lead in the introduction of a new order of things.*

Because the innovator has for enemies all those who have done well under the old conditions, and only lukewarm defenders in those who may do well under the new.

The larger the target customer, the more expensive the product, the slower first-time sales proceed. Truly disruptive technology (a category changer) is frequently greeted with disdain, caution, and roadblocks from the internal departments of hoped-for customers.

Some combination of "it wasn't invented here," or the ever-popular, "come back when you have ten referenceable customers we can talk with."

What does it take to succeed?

Quite close to what Jerry Garcia meant in a different context when he said, "You don't want to be the *best* at what you do, you want to be the *only* one." (Emphasis added.) A formidable challenge.

Goliath's highly deliberative go-to-market strategy was consistent with their long-term goals of gaining and holding market share over ten to twenty years. Whether significant sales happened in years one, two, or three was irrelevant: an unquestionably reasonable approach which had worked well for them historically.

Regrettably we weren't aware of *their* perspective when we entered the agreement. It all but guaranteed failure from *our* perspective.

Our remaining corporate cash was rapidly being depleted.

We were a super-small company (fewer than ten employees) funded solely by a now-exhausted base of high net worth individuals. They were unwilling to invest more without substantial evidence of commercial success.

We needed cash from sales *now*. The only market share timeframe we cared about was *today's*.

An Expectation Unarticulated is a Disappointment Guaranteed.

Shame on *us*.

Our unspoken assumption was Goliath knew how to introduce a product like ours to their customers. Given their century of commercial success, it would have felt presumptuous of our research and development startup to question their sales approach or go-to-market timing and tactics.

By the same token, shame on *them*.

Despite their sophistication and storied past, their unspoken assumption was we understood how *they* worked. They never considered or questioned whether dealing with an *external* product startup like us was any different from dealing with one of their successful *internal* product startups.

We were their first.

Neither David nor Goliath emerged covered with glory. An unspoken assumption-misalignment assured mutual unhappiness. The parting was amicable.

Soon afterward we signed a more limited distribution agreement with Aspiring Distributor. Their exclusive rights were limited to ten countries where we were able to verify their credibility and relationships with relevant customers.

Our diligence the second time through this process was more thorough and strategic. Our product would be the missing subcomponent in a larger system Aspiring was introducing to the marketplace. It was comforting knowing there were no alternative products satisfying their specifications.

Mutual vulnerability. 100% aligned interests.

Aspiring needed our solution in order to sell *their system*. We were their sole source supplier. We needed them to sell *our solution*. Our sole distributor.

Our importance to them was disproportionate to our size. The distribution agreement could be the Big Bang making them our "Potential Buyer."

Fast forward a year.

Many customer dogs were nibbling at our tantalizing technology. There was repeated testing and diligence, but no dog had purchased our dog food or Aspiring's system.

A single contract from the biggest dog would be upwards of $100 million. Up-and-Comer would soar. Without a contract (and only a few months of operating capital left), we wouldn't *survive* let alone *thrive*.

If this were a football game, we were in the red zone with prospective customers. We'd seemingly get to the ten-yard line, the five, the three, the two, the one ... but perpetually fail to get the ball across the sales goal line.

Not the prettiest of pictures for anyone.

With no cash and no customers our only alternative was to sell the business while still solvent and viable. There wasn't going to be a tulip-bulb, gold rush like Tennessee Technologies. No strategic buyer was going to approach us first. We were going to be sold, not bought.

My role and authority as Senior Strategic Advisor to Up-and-Comer was unusual: hire an investment banker and run and negotiate a sale of the company. I did *not* require board or stockholder approval for any decision facilitating a sale of the company.

That negotiating freedom let me reach binding agreements with a Buyer as Seller's ultimate decision-maker. Decisiveness. Certainty.

Based on the investment banker's pessimistic updates, it seemed increasingly unlikely we'd find a strategic industry purchaser. Prospects loved the technology's promise, but weren't convinced it was ready for commercial prime time.

Seven months of cash left.

Desperate times call for desperate measures. This required an orchestrated strategy unfolding over months in a series of highly designed steps.

Aspiring's agreement called for six months' advance notice to terminate their exclusive distribution rights.

Step 1. At a Director's meeting, I informed the board I was firing Aspiring Distributor, terminating their contract.

The Directors were *confused*. Eliminating your only sales channel partner, revenue source, and most probable buyer of your business isn't customary. It's closer to heretical or suicidal.

I laid it out very simply as a moment of truth, a forcing function. The only tactic to cause Aspiring to buy our company would be to cancel their distribution agreement with us; changing them from our *Potential* Buyer into our Buyer.

Although Aspiring Distributor repeatedly said they wanted to buy our business, I had no confidence they would do so in the normal course. Their conduct didn't match their words. They needed what I call an "Urgency Accelerator," a stimulus or trigger catalyzing a real fear of loss.

A Grateful Deadline?

Aspiring needed our subcomponent product in order to sell their system. Until there was a marketplace substitute product, their choices were limited:

- Develop an alternative,
- Buy *the solution* from us if we remained independent,
- Buy *us* (and control their own destiny), or
- buy our solution from whoever we sold the business to, and hope the buyer wanted to do business with them.

Step 2. Unable to set up my preferred format (a face-to-face meeting with Jack, Aspiring's CEO), I settled for the following phone conversation.

> **Me (to Jack):** "The board's decision to terminate your contract is tactical (not personal). No likely buyer wants to be stuck with you as their distributor. Firing you increases our value to many desirable counterparties.
>
> "You're super-smart. You'd do the same if the situation were reversed."

Pandering and groveling never go out of style.

> **Me (to Jack):**   "Because of your engaged efforts with the Big Dog, we can't terminate your right to sell our products in that country. We'll keep aggressively helping there because it's in our mutual interest.
>
> "That's the extent of our future *distribution* relationship."

Closing one door to open another.

> **Me:**   "Maybe we should explore a deeper, better relationship.
>
> "You're our most obvious corporate buyer because of the customer diligence and testing you've already been through.
>
> "Positive experience with Big Dog gives you real-world proof. You're the only one with early customer discussions going on in the four other countries you have experience in. You're the buyer who would benefit the most from acquiring us."

That's the set up to flipping apparent leverage by telling someone they *can't* buy you. The opposite of what you want to happen. Reverse psychology.

> **Me:**   "But Jack, at the price it would take to buy us quite frankly we don't think Aspiring can *afford* an acquisition. You don't have the cash, corporate will, or Director and stockholder intra-company alignment to do so."
>
> **Jack:**   "I'm the only *possible* buyer. This makes no sense."

> **Me:** "Jack, what makes you think you're the
> only possible Buyer? I'm *flabbergasted*."

I did not say he was *wrong*. I did not say there *were* other buyers. I simply said I was *flabbergasted*.

He was perceptibly shocked by the message.

Now he believed we weren't trying to persuade *him* to buy. He had to persuade *us* that Aspiring was even viable as a buyer if he wanted to remain in the acquisition discussion.

Everyone wants to be in the over-subscribed deal, to get into the club they can't get into. (Ask Groucho Marx.)

An Expectation Unarticulated is a Disappointment Guaranteed.

Merely articulating your expectation still doesn't guarantee you won't be disappointed.

Jack *articulated* his expectation he was the only buyer. He all but *shouted* negotiating leverage was his. His conclusion? He'd be able to purchase us at a bargain basement price.

Given our financial condition and limited exit opportunities, he was correct. Luckily, he didn't know that. This was high stakes poker and we had nothing but losing cards.

Time to turn the tables and use our weakness to advantage.

Poker players with busted hands sometimes bluff their way to victory. They confidently raise the ante and go "all-in," putting all their remaining chips on the table as a show of strength.

Since their counterparties can't see the cards which aren't turned over, the other players can't be 100% sure if the confidence displayed is genuine or feigned.

Uncertainty creates negotiating opportunity at a poker table or in a corporate finance deal as long as you don't reveal a "tell" (a physical or verbal action other players recognize as weakness). A facial tic. An artificial smile.

Cash is a proxy for time. Time is a proxy for opportunity.

We had none of them. No more cash. No more time. No more opportunity.

Our only remaining maneuver was introducing the threat of competition (and enhancing the appearance of scarcity) to shift perceived negotiating leverage from him to us.

The fear of competition is innate and powerful. Fear of missing out (FOMO). A fear someone else will buy what Buyer wants, and Buyer will be shut out.

If scarcity doesn't *exist*, self-help is recommended. *Create it.* ("We only choose one couple in each neighborhood to receive the *Universal Encyclopedia.* It's *exclusive.*")

Several months went by as we unsuccessfully continued trying to sell the business to others. Already-dim prospects were dimmer.

Jack called every several weeks. I never called him. I was playing hard to get.

> **Jack:** "We've progressed with the Big Dog and see interest from four other customers. You should reinstate our distributor relationship."

> **Me:** "Hope you're right about sales progress. You talk with the customers, not me, so you know and I don't."

Polite but unbending.

> **Me:** "Your news and views confirm our belief you'd benefit more than any other buyer. If you ever get serious about buying the company let me know. To be clear time is *not* in your favor."

Of course, it wasn't in ours either.

Though emotionally wearing, our disciplined stance was maintained for months.

There was now less than two months of cash in our bank account. Jack called but this time asking to meet for breakfast at a neutral site; not his office, not our office, and not at anyone's lawyer's office. A promising sign. (It must be important. He wanted to meet in person.)

Here's the exchange that occurred over a negotiating table disguised as a restaurant booth.

Jack (reaching into his coat pocket): "I have a signed Letter of Intent to hand you."

Me (to *myself*): "I've been in pet stores and I know this maneuver."

Me (to *Jack*): "Jack, *before* you give that to me, I want you to know your offer is too low *and* your offer is too low."

Jack (to me): "Marc, you haven't *seen* my offer yet. Why would you say that?"

Me (to Jack): "Well, your offer's too low because nobody puts their best offer on first. But your offer's *also* too low because you're valuing our business from a *defensive* posture. We're a key component in the larger system you sell, and you don't have an alternative supplier."

Said differently, they were trying to protect themselves against a specific vulnerability unique to them.

Me (to Jack):   "Any other bidder is looking for the *upside* value: global growth possibility, size of the total addressable marketplace, breadth of our product suite, and potential sales.

"They're looking to play *offense* rather than *defense,* so they inherently value our company more highly than you do.

"I repeat: your offer is too low *and* it's too low."

Structure unexamined is Stricture.

When we finally read the Letter of Intent from Aspiring, they offered to purchase all the company's *stock*, usually seller's preferred deal structure.

Imagine his surprise when my counterproposal was that they purchase only specific *assets* (essentially our trade secrets and intellectual property) plus assume *no* corporate liabilities.

Why?

In a normal stock purchase due-diligence process, we'd provide our financial statements, balance sheet, and tax returns.

Game over.

Aspiring would see we had *no cash* and *no time* and *no opportunity* for a conventional acquisition process. Jack's analysis was on the mark. If Aspiring delayed two more months we'd run out of cash and be forced to sell to them for virtually nothing.

In Impala (the bank-forced distressed sale) we took advantage of the normal lengthy acquisition document process. Unlike competing bidders, we shortened negotiation time (and increased deal probability) by skipping a Letter of Intent, and going directly to providing final documentation.

We didn't have even an Impala amount of time.

Purchasing assets typically involves as much (or more) paperwork than buying stock. We needed a trouble-free, short contract (not requiring us to reveal our financial position) permitting a deal to be negotiated and closed before we ran out of money.

How to turn necessity into virtue?

Things would be so much easier if Potential Buyer weren't buying an entire company. Maybe they weren't?

Salient fact: Up-and-Comer's commercial function was exclusively research and development. We made no direct sales.

Jack's company had intentionally shielded us as much as possible from direct contact with customers-in-process and the commercial marketplace. They didn't want their customers to realize who we were and how dependent they were on our expertise and innovation.

All these facts suggested we could turn their shield into our sword.

Framed from this perspective it wasn't hard to convince Jack that Aspiring Distributor didn't need disclosure from us about our historical sales, revenue prospects, or sales leads. Every sale had been made through them. Every revenue prospect and sales lead was in their possession and control, not ours.

With the exception of the full extent of our intellectual property, technology, know how, trade secrets, and applied-for-but-not-yet-granted patents, Jack and Aspiring knew more about our business and its future value than we did.

Bottom line?

Under the guise of limiting Buyer's liability (decreasing their risk by not making them purchase stock), the two of us agreed all the deal needed was modest documentation matching a modest purchase price. A six-page Assignment of Seller's Patents and Intellectual Property, plus a few employment agreements with the handful of our employees Buyer chose. (We would be able to pay off our bank loan and trade creditors but not much more.)

No need to title or treat this as an "Acquisition Agreement" as if Buyer were purchasing a fully fleshed out, operating company. Reality was much less grandiose.

I also reluctantly volunteered an essential fact Buyer had no way of knowing without access to our financial statements. After years of non-stop losses, we had an enormous net operating loss for tax purposes, larger than any possible purchase price.

That eliminated adverse tax considerations stemming from a typical stock purchase, alleviating (I hoped) any potential suspicions about why we proposed this structure. A benefit to them with no cost to us.

A week passed before we received Buyer's revised draft of the document we sent them. Jack and I met again.

> **Me:** "I'm confused. In my *right hand* I have 200 pages of documents from your lawyers. I didn't read any of the 194 pages they added. Clearly those were intended for the acquisition of Google by Amazon so I received them by mistake."

Sarcasm has its place in any negotiating arsenal.

> **Me:** "In my *left hand* is the six-page agreement reflecting the all-day, sweaty negotiations you and I had in a cramped, interior conference room.
>
> "You agreed you *weren't* buying an entire, ongoing company. You were fundamentally acquiring a limited asset, our technology and intellectual property.
>
> "Here's the question: Is your law firm trying to buy some undisclosed company, or are you trying to acquire all the relevant value from this company?
>
> "Good luck to your law firm as they try to find a seller willing to sign these documents. It just won't be me."

We closed on our six-page agreement (expanded by five pages) about three weeks before we ran out of money. Sweaty palms. Sleepless nights.

We made the best lemonade we could with available lemons. There's not enough sugar in this world to make really good lemonade from really bad lemons.

Let's move to an incredibly lucrative financial outcome arising from a toxic circumstance where orthodox tactics and process also might not have prevailed.

Chapter 9 Key Takeaways

- No matter how experienced (or conservative) the entrepreneur, the startup projections will be wrong about the amount of time and cash needed to succeed. They'll need more capital. They'll need more time. *Full stop.*

Startups are time, cash, and emotion vampires.

- Running out of cash has many negatives and no positives. You run out of time to create, iterate, sell your *products,* and grow your company.

You run out of time to sell the *business* itself through an orderly process. Bad exits are par for the underfunded course.

Cash is a proxy for time; time is a proxy for opportunity.

- If you're financially weak and vulnerable (no corporate time or cash) your most impactful gambit may be a business sales process behaving as if you're the *opposite*: strong and invulnerable.

When you have nothing to lose, there's nothing to lose. That should translate to freedom of action and invite theater.

- If deals start to drift, inform the lagging counterparty (clearly and politely) that if they don't act *now* and quicken their pace, you're going in another (unspecified) direction. Invoke an Urgency Accelerator.

You don't need to share that your unspecified direction may be bankruptcy. Some things are best left unsaid.

CHAPTER 10

A "SIMPLE TWIST OF FATE" IPO

It's instinctive to think of deals as if they were binary, a toggle switch turning a light either on or off. It's more productive to think of them as *non-binary*, as rheostats whose dimmers adjust light sources through an infinite range from dimmer to brighter.

In M&A transactions involving two corporations, the norm is black and white, buying or selling 100% of a business. There's not much gray in between.

But what if deal rheostats existed?

On to the wacky world of Wall Street.

Politics (as well as entrepreneurial companies) can make strange bedfellows. Women and men drawn together for a specific economic purpose, but little else in common.

All that binds investors putting up substantially all the equity to back a startup entrepreneur and management team may be a shared evaluation of future financial prospects. Rickety, unstable bonding compared to mission-driven businesses whose shared passion is planet-saving manufacturing.

Purely economic partners don't perpetually get along and fissures may develop. Groups forged from one-time motives may not hold together. They're welded, not 3D-printed. Operating differences and business philosophies develop and diverge over time.

Lack of "Sustainable DealGlue" leads to ruptures (not raptures), which is more or less what we'll see happened to Ruth's Retail. The startup investors ("Money Investors") who owned roughly half the company engaged an investment banker to sell the business.

That's not so unusual.

What *is* unusual is they did so *secretly* without consulting Ruth, the CEO-operator who owned the balance of the business.

When she learned about this through industry scuttlebutt it "didn't sit well." Her trusted strategic financial advisor introduced Ruth to me for legal counsel. Within moments of our first meeting, she vented justifiable frustration and anger, and gave me the entire background.

> **CEO to Me:** "I've built this company from nothing. Now they're trying to sell it out from under me. How much can we sue them for?"
>
> **Me:** "Your thinking is spot-on. Suing them *would* stop a sale of the business. No buyer is trying to buy a lawsuit.
>
> "On the other hand, a lawsuit would also be,
>   distasteful,
>   exceedingly costly,
>   public,
>   make everyone involved look bad, and
>   damage the company's value.
>
> "Social media would eat this drama up.
>
> "Not clear to me how that's a win for *anybody*."
>
> **CEO:** "Then what do we do?"

My first reaction was "where's the pony?" With a floor so thickly covered with corporate poop there *had* to be a pony. Where could we find it?

The CEO's instinctive reaction to sue the Money Investors was understandable. Suing is dramatic and feels good momentarily. It's the legal equivalent of wielding The Hammer of Thor, an emotionally satisfying blunt instrument which can sometimes be employed to great effect.

A frequently observed limitation is that every problem *isn't* a nail. A hammer *isn't* the universal panacea. Rushing to sue forestalls even considering more nuanced choices. Maybe a scalpel could be used to better advantage?

We did an impromptu cost-benefit analysis of the Money Investors' forced-sale approach, trying to look through their eyes as well as our own.

The three of us reviewed the company's history from inception. I asked intentionally open-ended questions to gain the broadest understanding of the human issues and interpersonal dynamics involved. Important details.

- *Who* in the Money Investors' group was affiliated with each other prior to the transaction?
- *Who* led the deal?
- *Who* followed?
- *What* was everyone's mutual understanding?
- *When, Where,* and *How* had the investment deal come together?

As the tale unfolded, less-than-ideal interpersonal dynamics were revealed; some evident from the outset, some revealed only with the passage of time. Viewed through my eyes, this was *not* a marriage made in heaven.

Angry Leader of the Money Investors was indisputably their Alpha Male and Commander-in-Chief. He and our CEO "had a history."

This was as much a *personal* parting-of-the-ways as a desire for investment liquidity.

From an *impersonal* perspective the business was doing well and generating cash. CEO-Ruth wanted to invest cash flow back into the business to grow. The Money Investors wanted to distribute cash flow to investors. Ruth's strategy focused on expanding the business. Theirs focused on cutting costs.

Both reasonable game plans but mutually exclusive.

Selling the business would accomplish what the CEO highlighted as the Money Investors' fundamental goals: getting *cash* and getting *out*. They'd have the cash they *did* want and get rid of the CEO they *didn't* want.

Money Investors' benefits were clear. Costs seemed prohibitively steep.

An operating business is devalued if a potential buyer knows the operator-CEO (not to mention a major stockholder) doesn't want to sell, particularly if the buyer wants CEO to continue driving the business's growth after acquisition.

How would that be apparent?

Any buyer performing diligence would get their information about the company's performance and prospects from unhappy management. Would it surprise you if a peeved CEO portrayed the business negatively to scare buyers away rather than entice them to stay?

Bottom line?

Fewer buyers would bid. The amount they'd be willing to pay would be less.

As a result of their tactics, the Money Investors would probably sell their stock, but it would be at a significant discount to achievable value in a well-conducted, unified sale. They'd hurt themselves as well as everyone else.

Now let's think about the cost-benefit of suing through the *CEO's* eyes.

CEO benefits were clear. Costs seemed steep.

The obvious benefit of litigation was preventing a sale she hadn't approved, effectively "punishing" the transgressing stockholders. The costs were mutually destructive, costing a fortune in time, lawyer's fees, and bad publicity.

If there was a pony it was well hidden. Could all concerned have their carrot cake and eat it too?

Oddly enough, yes: through an initial public offering (IPO).

In an IPO, Ruth's Retail would get cash by selling some newly issued corporate stock directly to the public (a *primary* sale). She could deploy those funds to support her growth strategy.

In the first step of a two-step process, Money Investors could simultaneously get cash by selling some (but maybe not all) of their stock directly to the public (a *secondary* sale).

By custom and contract, Money Investors couldn't sell any of their remaining stock for six months after the IPO, i.e., Wall Street's conventional "lockup period" for insiders. They could sell their stock then in the marketplace—a second step that would achieve the complete liquidity they wanted *plus* separation from the CEO.

On the other side of the corporate coin, the CEO didn't intend to sell any stock at the IPO or later. She wanted to bet on herself. With Money Investors gone she'd have controlling ownership. That outcome became a key part of the company's IPO narrative to prospective investors.

This initial public offering strategy would require two choreographed steps rather than the single step of a sale to fully succeed, but everyone would win.

Right-sizing an IPO

Our reaction to the Money Investors' secrecy was to be equally secretive. We designed a conceptually sound solution. Concepts are wonderful, but they weren't worth discussing with Money Investors unless the plan could be executed. Proposing a peace treaty that can't be implemented or honored is purposeless.

Ruth's Retail was an exciting company, and CEO-Ruth played well to crowds. We sought confirmation that an IPO was doable and met with a dozen major investment bankers. Our extremely unscientific question was whether we could raise a $100 million IPO. The amount was relatively random. No science behind it.

In return we received a dozen proposals to raise *exactly* $100 million. No questions asked.

Out of the mouth of babes

Late on a Sunday night a twenty-six-year-old Hong Kong-based investment banker called me. (Then he was the most junior member of a Global Top 5 investment-banking team. Now he's a world-wide respected financial guru.)

Young Investment Banker:	"Marc, I have an idea to explore and didn't want to wait until Monday morning."
Me:	"Fabulous. But please be quick I'm about to go to sleep."
Young Investment Banker:	"You said you wanted the company to raise $100 million. That's doable but an unattractively small IPO.
	"Executing that size raise won't create genuine liquidity either for your folks or (more importantly) for new institutional investors.
	"Let's raise *$200 million.*"
Me:	"I don't get it. If it's super hard to raise *$100 million* (which is what your partners tell us) why would we try to raise *$200 million*?
	"Logic tells me that's *twice* as hard?"
Young Investment Banker:	"Well, logic may always be *logical*, but that doesn't mean that it's always *right*. A $200 million deal really is at least twice as easy."

His suggestion was completely counterintuitive to me, but his explanation was convincing and (ultimately) correct.

Our overarching goal was separating the disgruntled stockholders from the CEO. It had nothing to do with a specific amount being raised for the company or any intended use of proceeds.

What he interpreted correctly was that raising a $100 million IPO was merely a tactical means to an end, not the goal.

By raising a larger, *more* liquid $200 million offering, more critically important institutional investors (mutual funds) would participate (and buy in larger amounts) than in a less liquid $100 million offering.

The bigger the offering, the larger the public "float" of SEC-registered stock sold, the more IPO-stock institutions could buy. They'd be comfortable knowing they could later re-sell their investment positions without huge price disruption.

In plain terms, there's a buyer for every seller, no matter how large the quantity of stock being sold.

An added deal benefit to increasing the offering was letting the Money Investors fully exit their offering on the IPO date. They wouldn't have to wait an additional six months after the IPO to be completely bought out.

In effect he did the same thing for us that we had done to respond to the Money Investors' unspoken ask. He correctly translated our spoken "ask" into the better "ask" we would have made if we were more sophisticated and better informed.

Everyone else mechanically solved the problem within the box-as-presented (i.e., executing a $100 million deal). Instead, he figured out what our request *should* have been if we'd known more, drawn a better box, and then executed inside it.

His firm ultimately won the deal (and my eternal admiration) by identifying our *real* need (separation from the Money Investors) rather than the *stated* need (raising capital to support sales growth).

The fire in my backyard wasn't from the barbecue

The Young Investment Banker's call was timely. Now we knew our solution could be executed. Less than a week later the Angry Leader of the Money Investors caught word of what we were doing.

(The "wall" in Wall Street isn't famed for being leak proof. Our visits with the Deal Dozen were predictably followed by market chatter.)

INDUSTRY TIP: As soon as more than one person knows a secret, it isn't.

He called me on a super-hot, summer Saturday morning to demand an immediate meeting. Muggy and buggy. Unusual for San Francisco.

My wife wasn't home. I was alone with our two small children. If he wanted an *immediate* meeting it had to be at my house.

Perfect!

A one-on-one, face-to-face, meeting on my turf, with enough lead time for me to set the stage and frame the message. Far superior to a group session with other principals and lawyers present as a distracting audience being played to.

Maybe, maybe, maybe in a solo setting Angry Leader could hear what I was saying. That freedom permitted me to express some views more authoritatively and directly than would have been possible in a gaggle of people. His loyal followers wouldn't feel compelled to rush to their leader's defense.

Structure unexamined is Stricture.

The few minutes between phone call and visit let me place two outdoor patio chairs close together in my driveway. ***Propinquity counts.***

After sitting down he yelled for about a half-hour with no pauses for social niceties or seemingly even breath. What he said was (more-or-less):

Angry Leader: "There's no way in hell *I'm* deviating from the path *I'm* on. We're selling Ruth's Retail whether you and the CEO like it or not.

"Expletive. Expletive. Expletive."

He had served our country well. As a former Army Ranger he displayed an almost encyclopedic knowledge of "colorful" word choices.

As loud and harsh as they were, however, he wasn't in the top 10% of the worst names I'd been called selling encyclopedias door-to-door. He wasn't even *close* to being the loudest. And he didn't throw anything at me. (Life was good.)

You've probably noticed how anger and frustration distort people's judgment. We were so close I could see biochemical changes occurring. Blood rushed to his face. His neck tightened. His jaw jutted. Classic fight behavior. Even if you didn't know the exact science behind what was happening, you could still discern the impact.

I listened intently and said *nothing.*

Nodded my head up and down several times to confirm I was hearing what he was saying. I didn't want to further enrage him by remaining silent and physically unresponsive. In his agitated state he might misconstrue silence to mean that I was ignoring him. (People *hate* to be ignored.)

Finally, he paused. Exhaustion? Dehydration? (I had "forgotten" to offer him something to drink.)

Me:	"Anything else you want to say?"
Angry Leader:	"You're damned right there is."
Me:	"OK. Go ahead. Say it."
Angry Leader:	"Expletives. Curse words. #*#!**......"
Me:	"Are you done now?"
Angry Leader:	"No!"
Me:	"Great. Keep talking."

He finally stopped berating me after what seemed like another hour (but certainly wasn't).

In other circumstances (or with a different counterparty) I might have tried lightening the mood by responding with humor. People are more genuine and open when laughing, often helpful to a dialogue or negotiation. People relax and let their guard down.

This meeting was too precarious and volatile to take any chance that my irrepressible sense of humor might not be appreciated. That prevented me from saying any of the following thoughts that raced through my brain and stayed there.

My *repressed* humor:	"I'm *guessing* here now. Work with me. Are you telling me you're not a happy camper? I want to make sure I'm not overthinking this."
	Or ...
	"*Wow.* That was *impressive.* I hope it was *impromptu* and you didn't spend a lot of time rehearsing."
	Or ...
	"Frankly, I'm disappointed. I went to school with kids from Flatbush with a much wider range of four-letter words."

My actual quiet, restrained response lasted no more than ninety seconds. I lowered my voice to barely above a whisper. He leaned forward to hear me. (Shifting negotiating control from him to me).

Me:	"Thank you for sharing. That was informative.
	"Your group has a legitimate right to exit your investment and achieve liquidity. I acknowledge and respect that.
	"You're right: economic partnerships don't have to last forever. Bad partnerships are bad for everyone.
	"I completely agree you and the CEO have irreconcilable views of how to run this business."

My comments were neutral. They favored no one and disrespected no one. They acknowledged what he said, confirmed I'd heard him, and then agreed with (and explicitly validated) as many of his points as was possible.

I did *not* question the propriety of him trying to unilaterally sell the business. No righteous indignation, moralizing, or scolding on behalf of the CEO as aggrieved party.

Histrionics are overrated

Consider the alternatives.

I could have returned *his* fiery speech with *my* fiery speech and yelled back at full volume. That seemed likely to turn into a pernicious ego contest with two losers and no winners. ("I'm as tough as you are, you ****##!!**")

Instead, I thought about the unpretentious words a friend of mine uses to start many discussions: "What's the desired outcome?"

A high-decibel, mudslinging contest wasn't in the top fifty choices.

My desired outcome was utilizing this out-of-the-blue, one-on-one, encounter to convert him. In my perfect world he would endorse the IPO path believing it represented the best outcome for his Money Investors, *not* because it represented the best path for the CEO and the company.

Alignment.

Sophisticated, high-stakes corporate transactions are well served by calm environments facilitating detached analysis. Let everyone thoughtfully assess where their own self-interest and mutual self-interest lies.

A deliberate part of my style is reducing friction to the irreducible minimum. Win only what you need to win. You don't need to win everything in sight. Yelling may be momentarily satisfying (sort of like suing) but more-often-than-not it creates unhelpful short-term, intermediate, and long-term friction.

I *de*-escalated the verbal volume, changed the one-sided, throbbing rhythmical *flow*, and "un-riled" the negotiations.

Having thanked him for sharing his feelings and version of the facts, I shared the economic logic, timetable, and preliminary valuations of the proposed IPO. ("The process is well underway. We'll be public less than two months from now.") There was no edge in my voice or adversarial intonation.

Wall Street's consensus was the Money Investors would receive boatloads more money through an IPO than they would from selling the entire company.

> **Me:** "Just for clarity. Would you rather make *less* money by forcing a sale of the company under fractious, controversial circumstances, *or* go public with a united front and make *more* money?"

Like many fruitful questions this was rhetorical. He didn't respond because he couldn't respond without sounding ridiculous, even to himself. The question answered itself.

What could he possibly say?

> **Angry Leader** (hypothetical response): "I'm *so* mad and *so* stupid I'd rather make *half* the profit doing it my way instead of *double* the profit doing it yours."

He undeniably agreed with me though pride wouldn't permit immediate acceptance. I would have won. He would have lost. A proud man would have lost face. That was never going to happen.

Instead he temporized and bought time.

> **Angry Leader** (much less angry): "Everything IPO-related must be approved by *my* personal accountant. *My* accounting firm will be the company's accountants until the IPO *closes*. I want their name on any SEC filings."

Said differently, he did agree with me but avoided saying so.

The outcome?

And they all lived happily ever after.

Wait. No. That's a different story.

In *this* epic the "road show" (investment banker-organized investor meetings) was hugely successful. Demand for Ruth's Retail stock increased daily. The proposed offering price rose sharply. Adam Smith strikes again.

Most deals have twists and turns, unexpected, vertigo-inducing moments. Emotional rollercoasters. Shortly before the SEC effective date for the IPO this unanticipated dialogue occurred:

Formerly **Angry Leader of the Money Investors:**	"This IPO is going splendidly. The boys and I have been talking. We'd be leaving a lot of money on the table if we sold at the IPO price. We're going to hang on to *all* our shares and not sell them for a while."
Me (incredulously):	"Sorry. I must have lost my train of thought for a minute. Could you just repeat that last sentence again?"
Formerly **Angry Leader of the Money Investors** (with no apparent sense of irony):	"Sure. No problem. We'd be leaving a lot of money on the table if we sold at the IPO price. We're going to hang on to all our shares and not sell them for a while."

Greed and self-interest had supplanted fear in this deal roller coaster.

Me:	"That's really great to hear. I'm pleased you agree how successful our *joint* strategy has been."

It wasn't easy to refer to the public offering as "our *joint* strategy." I winced inwardly while maintaining a straight face outwardly.

> **Me:** "This capital raise is a remarkably beneficial response to your attempts to sell the company. We've more-than-satisfied your legitimate economic objectives.
>
> "Our CEO is Wall Street's newest star-of-the-moment. Understandably she can't forgive or forget what you did. The financial community love *her*, and have bought the fact that s*he* (not you and your group) will control Ruth's Retail after Closing.
>
> "To be clear, you're going to sell as much of your stock as the IPO marketplace will absorb."

After one-or-two(ish) more idyllic discussions that's what happened.

Ruth's Retail went public. The dissident Money Investors made a fortune. The CEO made a fortune *and* gained her corporate freedom.

Triumph snatched from the jaws of dysfunction and defeat; a curiously positive inversion of the Law of Unintended Consequences.

Let's move to a deal where being patient and polite demonstrated the more common *negative* impact of the same law.

Chapter 10 Key Takeaways

The obvious isn't always optimal, and the optimal isn't always obvious.

- Trying to unilaterally sell Ruth's Retail was an *obvious* (albeit blunt) solution of sorts for the unhappy Money Investors, which minimized their own financial results while simultaneously imperiling the company. Clearly *bad* news.

Good things happened when Team-Ruth immediately looked for a pony. The structure and consequences of a $100 million IPO was a winning solution better than the Money Investors' fractured sale.

Finding an adequate deal structure didn't stop Young Investment Banker from looking for an even better solution. Viable was his *floor*, not his *ceiling*.

Challenging a winning deal structure and outcome by increasing the offering from $100 to $200 million let all involved win even more. (By the merest of coincidences, it also doubled the investment bankers' fees. I'm just sayin'.)

- The optimal solution emerged through an adaptive, iterative process that started with dysfunctional irritation and an unhappy *obvious*, progressed to *adequate*, and battled to *optimal*.

Isn't that how pearls get started?

WITH DUE RESPECT TO THE ROLLING STONES, "TIME, TIME, TIME IS [NOT ALWAYS] ON YOUR SIDE, SIDE, SIDE"

Every deal has its own distinctive rhythm, cadence, and time signature. Hip hop, funk, blues, soul, metal, rap, electronic dance music, rock, jazz, classical, country western, or bluegrass.

Many of these styles merged to create the Grateful Dead's unique voice and voicing. Percussionist Mickey Hart said, "[t]here's nothing like music to relieve the soul and uplift it. Life is about rhythm."

Time plays a role in deals, music, and the physical universe. (Remember the Big Bang?) Our individual awareness of time, our idiosyncratic relationship with it, influences how we interact and communicate with deal counterparties.

Time can be your friend, foe, or ally, but its impact is rarely neutral. You can try to control and influence it with foresight and critical path planning, or fail to do so and passively accept its dictates.

Part of sophisticated dealmaking is knowing how to pull chestnuts out of a raging fire, but a Dealjammer's first choice is to not *be* in the fire. They plan obsessively to minimize the possibility that future actions or events will "derail" their deal.

Jack Welch (legendary CEO of General Electric) put it this way: "Control your own destiny or someone else will." I recommend the former, not the latter.

Deals, like the universe, tend toward entropy.

In the *physical* universe entropy is a gradual decline into disorder. The *fiscal-deal* universe mimics this concept.

If time elongates (think financially distressed Impala's seemingly endless informal auction), transaction momentum dissipates. Passage of time, by itself, is frequently your real deal enemy.

Every second a deal isn't closed increases the likelihood that it never will. Things or people outside your sight or dominion intervene. Deals fall apart and spin out of control.

Given time and opportunity to think, people (and as we'll see, banks) change their minds, invent "imaginary horribles," get distracted by other activities in their business or personal lives, or are swept away by macro factors such as September 11 or stock market crashes.

- People go on *vacation*. (How thoughtless!)
- People get *sick*. (How thoughtless!)
- People *forget* what they agreed to and why.
- People come to *regret* what they agreed to and later revise history in accordance with their regrets.

Deal conviction dims. *Seller's* remorse, *Buyer's* remorse, and *Lender's* remorse glow ever brighter. Deal-breaking forces all.

Deals with shared momentum close. Deals *without* it don't. Time management is a *tactic*. Time management is a *strategy*.

Time is the invisible but palpable enemy.

You *do* want to be able to jam, to improvise, and go with the flow. But you don't want to jam so long that the deal falls apart. The goal of negotiating isn't negotiating. The goal is achieving an outcome.

It's never over until it's over. You can bank on it.

Chickens shouldn't be counted until they're hatched. A deal isn't closed until it's closed *and* the check clears the bank.

An extreme example?

A transaction set to close at "money midnight" disintegrated at the last tick of the clock: 11 hours, 59 minutes, and 59 seconds.

Cinderella Corporation (a Los Angeles business I was involved with) imported electronics from Asia. They borrowed "gigundous" amounts of money from several west coast financial institutions. Each source independently provided a specialized form of unsecured, *short-term* financing commonly used in these kinds of businesses.

Cinderella was nicely profitable, well-run, and had a strong credit history: a highly desirable borrower. Interest rates on the financings were exceptionally low reflecting that. Each bank was competing with the others to be "allowed" to loan money.

After months of internal long-term, strategic planning meetings, our CFO was delegated to deliver versions of the following speech to each lender separately:

Cinderella's CFO:	"I'm going to make you an offer you won't want to refuse.
	"I want to pay higher interest *and* give you collateral to secure your loan (i.e., pledge our inventory, accounts receivable, and equipment to you)."
Bank #1:	"You're a funny guy. Unusual for a CFO. What's the catch?"
Cinderella's CFO:	"No catch.
	"We want to consolidate our separate *short-term, unsecured* debt facilities into a single, *long-term, secured* loan. Less subject to the changing whims of our capital suppliers. De-risk cash availability.
	"You'll each have the same loan amount you have now but with more downside protection and upside profitability."

Bank #1: "There *has* to be a catch. But my mother taught me to say 'thank you' graciously. I look forward to the paperwork."

The respective institutions all quickly said "yes" to the loan consolidation. Why not? They would each make more money with less risk. Not complicated.

We "made the sale" quickly (mere minutes). These weren't encyclopedias so we couldn't get the metaphorical bank checks and leave their financial houses.

Months passed documenting the consolidated transaction (New Loan). There was no clamor from us to hurry up since we continued borrowing under the old facilities and paying less interest than we would under the New Loan.

The Closing date was twice scheduled and twice cancelled due to a conflict for the smallest lender.

Eventually all participants gathered at a conference room board table designed to accommodate twenty directors. Dozens of documents. Borrower's officers and major owners spent three hours signing each one of them.

11:00 through 2:00.

Only slightly fewer documents needed to be signed by the Lead Bank, the designated "Agent" for the other three banks in the New Loan syndicate. Lead Bank dutifully signed them all.

2:00 through 4:15.

The last step to close required each of the other syndicate members to separately sign the one-page contract binding their respective institutions to the New Loan.

4:*16* and 4:*17*.

The *second* and *third* banks signed.

At 4:*18* the officer from the *fourth* (and final) participant picked up their pen (with the requisite blue ink). As if on cue a secretary entered and informed the remaining signer there was an urgent phone call for them.

4th Banker:	"Can you believe this? First time in more than five hours I have something to do.
	"Really sorry about this interruption. I'll be right back."
CFO:	"No problem. We'll be here. After months of delay, a few more minutes isn't going to hurt anything."

Fifteen minutes later the lender hadn't returned. Based on personal history, if *I* were the missing person, everyone would have assumed I'd gotten lost.

But it *wasn't* me.

Something had to be very, *very* wrong. Family emergency? Run on the bank? We were concerned *for* him and *about* him.

Whether the absence was excused or unexcused, the New Loan wouldn't be closed until he executed the remaining piece of paper. No one was leaving until that occurred.

At last, our *CEO* went to find out what was going on

Ten *more* minutes passed. It was verging on a half hour before our CEO and the banker returned together.

4th Banker (with ashen face):	"I don't know how to say this. That was the Chairman of my Board.
	"He revoked my authority to sign the loan documents. Our bank is *not* going to participate in the New Loan."
Everyone else:	"Say what?!"
4th Banker:	"Is it helpful for me to stay?"
Everyone else:	"*No.* Leaving as quickly as you can is an excellent idea."

No one ever learned what happened. None of us could conjure a scenario explaining the Chairman's timing or thought process. If the call had occurred seconds later, agreements would have been fully signed and the bank would have been contractually obligated under the New Loan.

A seemingly easy "done" deal, with all counterparties aligned, failed to close when only:

- a *single* signature was needed,
- from a *single* person,
- who was *sitting* with us at the Closing,
- *poised* to sign, and
- with a *pen in his hand.*

Six inches from Closing. 11 o'clock. 59 minutes. 59 seconds. A deal's never closed until it's closed. You can bank on it.

Coda (for the curious among you): We quickly found a replacement for the disappearing bank.

Fortunately, we didn't need the money on the original Closing date or this wouldn't be a (mostly) amusing story. Enormous economic damage could have occurred. (Imagine if we were using the New Loan to close an acquisition but we couldn't fund *our* deal because the bank didn't fund *theirs.*)

Used with intentionality, time can also be your tactical ally

Applying time pressure can be your friend, forcing priorities to emerge and decisions to be reached.

Fixed, finite time remaining for negotiations should cause DealCirclers to exclusively fight about objectively important stuff. *Less* important stuff gets resolved quickly and more easily. The difference between wheat and chaff suddenly becomes readily discernible.

A tax-driven, year-end deal started any day in *November* will close in less than two months (i.e., by December 31). Counterparties are similarly motivated and responsive to a genuine deadline.

The same deal started in *October* will probably take *three* months. The same deal started on *Labor Day weekend* has a strong chance of taking *four* months. Always closing by December 31.

People instinctively set a deal pace based on the perceived/real timeframe.

As one of my heroes (C. Northcote Parkinson) said, "Work expands to fill the amount of time available to get it done in." The shorter the timeframe, the faster people work, and the more they focus on palpably big issues.

They:

- work late without complaining,
- respond quickly to counterparty questions or requests,
- negotiate straight through weekends, and
- put unremitting pressure on internal or external roadblocks.

Question: How do you summon the unquestioned power of deadlines when one doesn't exist?

Answer: Create them (artificially if you need to) just as you created scarcity to sell an encyclopedia.

People respond when they have to. Authentic (or perceived) deadlines with impactful consequences alter/modify human behavior and collective actions of DealCirclers.

Countless deals have closed because:

- Buyer's team is going on their annual retreat *this weekend*, or
- Seller's CEO is leaving for vacation *next Tuesday*, or
- the *end of a fiscal quarter* reporting period for a public company is looming, or
- the bank commitment expires if a condition precedent hasn't been satisfied by *month-end*.

You've probably noticed a slew of lawsuits settling on the fabled courthouse steps (or in the judge's conference room) on the first day of a trial.

Why? Beginning the court action is an objective deadline. *Not* subjective. *Not* susceptible to control by the parties who are litigating. Inviting and leading to finality.

Generating speed and pressure is a deal *tactic*. Generating speed and momentum is a deal *strategy*. Generating momentum and closing is the *goal*.

Einstein on Dealjamming

Einstein's Theory of Relativity explains how space and time are linked for objects moving at a consistent speed in a straight line. (Think DealCircle counterparties.) He crushed it by observing that time is relative. (It's the fourth dimension.)

Unlike Einstein, my *personal* theory of relativity is best expressed this way.

Question: How do you make winter pass quickly in Cleveland?

Answer: Sign a 90-day note in December.

My family's theory of relativity (in all spaces and environments) is more rigid than either mine or Einstein's. Time everywhere is *railroad* time, not *restaurant* time. "Five minutes" means *precisely* five minutes.

If your Saturday night dinner reservation is for 8:45, most restaurants (except for the newest and hottest) will accommodate arrival anytime from 8:30 to 9:15. They won't give your table away even if you're "late" and the restaurant is crowded.

Restaurant time is easy to understand from *their* perspective. They're incented to be patient with you.

- If you aren't there, you can't order.
- If you don't order, you can't be served.

- If you're not served, you won't pay, and
- they won't get your money.

Railroad time is equally easy to understand from *their* perspective.

If you arrive at New York's Grand Central Station at 8:*55* for an 8:*45* railroad departure, the train won't be there.

Most of us know that from unpleasant experience. If you don't, consider yourself forewarned.

Why?

You already paid for a non-refundable ticket. The railroad *has* your money; they don't *need* you. They have no motivation to be patient or flexible. So they aren't.

The railroad's view of time is more than mere indifference. Their incentives are to be inflexible, not patient. Extending departure time to accommodate even one passenger wrecks the balance of the railroad system's schedule.

A delay leaving Station #1 makes the train late at Station #2. That misstep ripples throughout the balance of the railroad system's day. Passengers miss connections and are stranded and furious.

My family's view of time tends to be railroad-based. They're genuinely upset if we're going to arrive at 8:*47* for an 8:*45* dinner reservation. (As an act of charity, I'll spare you the analysis of whose watch governs.)

If our arrival won't be until 8:*49* (an unpardonable sin) we call the restaurant to explain not only the fact that we'll be a few minutes late, but also why.

Legitimate, disparate views of time by DealCirclers affects transactions. What would you expect if your counterparty tells you *today* (at noon) to expect their written response *tomorrow*?

Railroad-type negotiators get concerned if their counterparty's response isn't there at 9:30 the following morning.

Railroad-type negotiator (to their colleagues):	"I mean it's '*tomorrow!*' Where's the response?"

If the reply hasn't arrived by 2 o'clock that afternoon, they're close to panic.

Railroad-type negotiator (to their colleagues):	"What do you think the problem is? Did we press too hard? Should we take some demands off the table?"

If the reply isn't there by 5 o'clock, the deal is indisputably dead.

#1 Deal Worrywart:	"What does it mean?"

#2 Deal Worrywart:	"Has the deal fallen apart?"

#1 Deal Worrywart:	"What are they trying to *tell* us????"

#2 Deal Worrywart:	"How can we get this deal *back* on track?"

I'm more of a *restaurant*-type negotiator.

Tomorrow could mean breakfast, lunch, end-of-business, or slightly before midnight the following day. It's super-easy to overhear someone's directional intent as promise.

In restaurant-speak (not railroad-speak) your counterparty's "tomorrow" could reflect the following (wholly internal) thought process:

Counterparty:	"This document is important, and this deal is important.
	"I'll give my reply higher priority than usual and take less than a full week before responding."

Deal WorryWart or not, systems and people aren't perfect. Why take chances? Be explicit. Get in rhythm with your DealCirclers.

#1 Deal Worrywart (to counterparty):	"That's great, Sue. We look forward to receiving the documents tomorrow by 10:00 a.m., New York time.
	"It's summer here so we're on EDT, three hours earlier than you on the west coast. Let us know if that's going to be a problem. Otherwise we'll assume we're in synch."

With expectations firmly set, Deal Worrywarts *might* reasonably start worrying if something promised to arrive at an agreed time is objectively late, and wonder what that means.

Maybe your counterparty is using time *tactically*. Maybe they're *intentionally* varying the deal's rhythm and tempo to increase pressure on you, creating uncertainty and anxiety at your end.

Those are ideas worth thinking about. Of course, it goes without saying that it's also not a bad idea to double-check your junk filter.

In the next chapter we'll see more reasons to give your counterparty the benefit of "bad communication doubt" (at least once or perhaps twice) by considering words of wisdom from noted deal theorist, George Bernard Shaw.

Chapter 11 Key Takeaways

- Even though it's invisible, Dealjammers are always aware of and can *feel* the value, power, and danger of *time*. Used to advantage, time is a dealmaker's greatest ally. Ignored or under-managed the passage of time is a transaction's biggest enemy.

A body not in motion trends toward falling apart.

- Time pressure combined with meaningful deadlines (analytical or emotional, genuine or artificial) is *the* secret to deals getting done or not.

The DealCircle is highly interdependent. Like a railroad system, negative consequences ripple from seemingly insignificant delays.

If a deal loses momentum (even briefly), it's less likely to close. Seller's or Buyer's remorse set in. Macro events occurring outside the sight or control of Seller or Buyer torpedo transactions. Not many deals closed on September 12th.

- Dealjammers (buyer or seller) actively and relentlessly push their own team and intermediaries (as well as the counterparty's) to get deals done as fast as humanly possible ... and frequently faster.

Speed is a tactic. Speed is a strategy.

- Deals are never over until they're over. Repeat after me. Deals are never over until they're over.

GOD GAVE YOU ONE MOUTH AND TWO EARS. THE RATIO WASN'T AN ACCIDENT

Playwright, music critic, and journalist George Bernard Shaw said it best. "The single biggest problem with [human] communication is the illusion that it has occurred."

That reality endangers every deal. The more DealCirclers there are, the more probable that defective human communication will slowly poison a transaction.

Have you played the broken telephone game? Words are whispered from each participant to the next. The last recipient says out loud what they heard. End results bear no relationship to the original input.

The same phenomenon occurs with lyrics in well-known songs, which have persistently been misheard and then repeated as gospel.

Artist/Group:	Lyrics as *Written*	Lyrics as *Heard*
Elton John	Hold me closer tiny dancer.	Hold me closer Tony Danza.
Taylor Swift	Got a long list of ex-lovers.	All the lonely Starbucks lovers.
Credence Clearwater	There's a bad moon on the rise.	There's a bathroom on the right.

Let any of those songs be your earworm as we move to the next story. (Don't thank me now, you can thank me later!)

Communication is a *system*. One (or more) people are sending information. One (or more) are paying attention and hearing information. At both ends, the communication needs to be clear and effective to be heard as intended.

Here's a quintessential illustration:

Behemoth Buyer was trying to purchase Grand Canyon Group, owned by a handful of stockholders. In preliminary discussions their CEO insisted we purchase all the *stock* of the company.

You're already familiar with numerous reasons (starting with liability avoidance) that acquirors (like us) generally prefer buying *assets*. They don't want responsibility for Seller's obligations (known, unknown, or unknowable) unless they're specifically assumed and accepted by Buyer.

In this instance, twenty-first-century business sensibilities hadn't really taken hold at Seller. We had (perhaps unfounded) sensitivities around a few areas. Taxes. Pension plans. Sexual harassment.

Deal momentum was slow-moving and unfocused. Financial statements and possible deal structures and terms had been exchanged.

Anything else?

- LOTS of phone calls between *principals*,
- LOTS of phone calls between *lawyers*, and
- LOTS of phone calls between *accountants*.

The early winner in this deal was AT&T.

We were far from the take-it-or-leave-it stage. Grand Canyon was highly profitable. No deadlines or time pressures impacting them or us. Agreement might/might not be reached from this disjointed negotiation among friendly but chippy competitors.

In an attempt to expose deal differences and narrow gaps, all DealCirclers met. The aggressive agenda was reaching consensus on *major* economic variables (structure and price) plus as many *minor* issues as could be resolved. This wasn't intended as a final negotiation session.

The first two hours were a verbal slugfest. Toe-to-toe. Eyeball-to-eyeball. Was this going to be a purchase of assets or stock? If we couldn't coalesce around basic structure, then no deal was doable.

Seller's CEO— *Majority* Stockholder:	"Grand Canyon's owners are unanimous. This has to be a Stock Purchase. After Closing, you'll own everything we currently own involving the business.
	"You'll get all profits from ongoing operations. It's only common sense you'll also take all business liabilities, past or present. *Symmetry.*"
Buyer's CEO (with a broad smile):	"What a coincidence! We're only willing to buy specific assets and assume specific liabilities. This *has to be* an Asset Purchase.
	"You've made all profits from the business through Closing. It's only common sense any liabilities we don't specifically assume from operations prior to Closing, will remain yours. *Symmetry.*"
Seller's CEO-*Majority* Stockholder:	"Seller's stockholders are *united*. Either you buy *stock*, or there's no deal."
Buyer's CEO (*still* with a broad smile):	"Again, a remarkable coincidence! "Buyer's stockholders and management are *united* on this issue. Either we buy *assets* or there's no deal."

Seller's *Minori-ty* Stockholder (with an aggressive frown):	"Are you saying this is a deal killer?"
Me:	"Those aren't words I ever use. "That said, structure is so important there's not much to discuss if we can't all align on this issue."
Seller's lawyer:	"Can we borrow an empty conference room to talk among ourselves?"
Seller's lawyer (returning 30 minutes later):	"My clients *agree* this will be an *asset* purchase paid in cash plus a subordinated note."

Minority stockholder was visibly sullen but stayed.

After every negotiating session I summarize major points agreed-to (or identified for later discussion and resolution). It had been a productive day, and several dozen matters (major and minor) had been ironed out.

- **Purchase Price.** $60 million.
- **Deal Structure.** Asset purchase.
- **Manner of Payment.** $50 million cash at Closing, plus a $10 million *fully subordinated* promissory note (Deal Note).

The basic form and substance of the promissory note was deal standard. For practical purposes these type of notes constitute an interest-bearing loan from "Seller-as-Lender" to "Buyer-as-Borrower." Subordination to Buyer's bank is conventional but less standard.

Notwithstanding, all DealCirclers were sophisticated, seasoned negotiators. There was no reason to believe there was the slightest ambiguity in our exchanges. That never stops me. I went through my normal session-ending drill.

Predictable. Boring. Important.

> **Me:** "OK with everyone if I summarize to-day's results?"

> **Seller's Deal-Circle** (nodding their heads up and down in agreement): "Absolutely. It's been a long day."

Because structure had been *the* deal-breaking issue ten hours earlier, my summary began with what was intended as a joke about the one issue that unequivocally *didn't* need to be cleared up.

> **Me:** "And, of course, it's an *asset* purchase."

> **Everyone** (*except* for Seller's Minority Stockholder): General laughter, and even some wry smiles.

> **Seller's *Minority* Stockholder:** "No, that's *not* what was agreed; it's a *stock* purchase."

Everyone on the *buy* side was *stupefied*.

This wasn't faulty hearing or innocent misunderstanding. Minority stockholder simply announced his original position as if the intervening hours and agreements hadn't occurred.

Everyone on the *sell* side was *livid*.

Millions of dollars had conceptually and emotionally passed from Buyer to Sellers during the day. By late afternoon it was clear Seller's owners had mentally started spending their money.

The sun was setting on the day but we hoped not on the deal. A fractious hour ensued before reaching agreement (for the second time) that Buyer was purchasing assets not stock.

Minority Stockholder's backtracking increased my caution meter. My day's-end summary immediately got longer and more granular than normal. Unexpectedly useful because the following conversation unfolded.

> **Me:** "Just confirming. The $10 million Deal Note we owe you as part payment of the purchase price will be *fully* subordinated to our Bank loan."

Seller's lawyer "We never agreed to that."
(matter-of-factly):

Now I was disturbed and authentically confused.

A new DealCircler (Buyer's lender) metaphorically joined the negotiations. Why hadn't they appeared before? Because our loan agreement was super-clear.

We didn't need bank's approval to make this acquisition or borrow closing funds, *but* we couldn't issue DealDebt like the $10 million note unless it was "fully subordinated" to the bank's loan as the bank defined the term.

The only exception was if the bank consented to less than full subordination. (For the record, they *never* consented.)

Seller's lawyer was excellent; solidly understood law, business, and economics. A real pro. Her exceptional interpersonal skills were a key factor in facilitating agreement and maintaining an overall cordial negotiating environment.

> **Me:** "We absolutely *did* agree."

Seller's lawyer: "We absolutely did *not*."

Unlike Minority Stockholder, her objections weren't negotiating noise or selective memory. I listened harder, trying to discern the implications and origin of every word she was saying.

Me (volunteering an approach forward):	"My line-by-line, annotated notes from today indicate we reached multiple agreements about the four ways the Deal Note was subordinated.
	"Collateral. Principal. Interest."
Seller's lawyer:	"Yes, yes, and yes."
Me:	"The fourth subordination variable is hyper-technical.
	"If we (Buyer) miss a payment under the Deal Note, you can't sue us and force the entire amount of the note to be immediately payable without our lender's permission."
Seller's lawyer:	"*No*. We never agreed to that."

Lewis Carroll's *Alice in Wonderland* springs to mind:

Humpty Dumpty:	"When I use a word it means just what I choose it to mean—neither more nor less."
Alice:	"The question is whether you can make words mean so many different things."

To be clear, neither of us was trying to pull a Humpty Dumpty.

Knowing the bank's interpretation, when I said the note was *fully* subordinated it was meant literally, i.e., the note was subordinated in each and every possible economic and contractual respect.

She fairly interpreted *fully subordinated* as subordinating the Deal Note only as to collateral and payment of principal and interest. Huge negatives to Seller and many would agree with her that this constituted full subordination. (Unfortunately our bank wouldn't. This was concrete. Not abstract.)

After meticulously retracing this back-and-forth dialogue, the fault line creating the communication failure was revealed.

Despite all being in the same room, physically uttering the same words (full subordination), listening to those same words, in good faith, we recorded the messages and meanings differently.

Another forty-five minutes passed once again negotiating an important issue mutually believed to have been fully negotiated seven hours earlier.

By day's end this deal was back on track.

Would it have been derailed if we hadn't collectively re-confirmed the:

- deal's *structure* (stock), and
- extent (absolutely *full*) of the note's *subordination?*

Maybe. Maybe not. If Seller had reason to mistrust us at this early stage, and on such a "clear" issue, how could they trust us on any other aspect of deal process and outcome?

The minimum deal damage would have been delay, interpersonal friction, and decreased probability of Closing. We would have riled them up when the goal was to *"un-rile"* them.

Establishing "Sustainable Deal Empathy" is a method Dealjammers employ to keep a deal and DealCircle together. Without uncovering the subordination misunderstanding we'd have created the opposite. *Un*sustainable *Deal Antipathy*. Not cool.

Songbird meeting

You can't overstate how easily counterparties fail to communicate, and the mischief thereby unleashed.

I'm frequently the Senior Strategic Advisor to early-stage companies. (And, *no*, I don't know what a Senior Strategic Advisor is or does any more than you do.) On the other hand, I was a Director of Songbird and I *do* know what a Director is and does.

We received an investment term sheet from a prominent early-stage venture capital fund that routinely funded young companies. Like their compatriots, they took high risks and expected commensurately high returns and corporate control.

Customarily we'd have modified their term sheet, inserted language and substance we were willing to agree to, and returned it to them with a polite cover letter.

Small problem. This term sheet was flat-out philosophically (not financially) unacceptable.

Our corporate facts were the opposite of many of the Fund's investments where passive boards were studded with handpicked friends and relatives of unseasoned entrepreneurs.

By contrast Songbird had seasoned management and battle-scarred Directors who met monthly. The entire board committed substantial time, treasure, and talent to the business.

Management checks and balances were ample.

Other than the investment amount (which we agreed with) and the introductory paragraph and description of the Fund (which we were indifferent to), every sentence in the Term Sheet would have to be rewritten. Probably not productive, and verging on insulting.

Time to put on a "Dealjammer's Empathy Hat" and look through the Fund's eyes trying not to let our own needs color the view.

I called their lead negotiator. Not a text. Not an email. A person-to-person call.

Me:	"Why don't we meet in my home office to informally talk through the deal. Help me understand your proposed terms, and what you're trying to accomplish."
Lead Negotiator:	"Marc, our term sheet speaks for itself. Let's just talk on the phone."
Me:	"I would really, really, really appreciate it if you'd humor me."

> **Lead Negotiator** (noticeably *un*enthusiastically): "I'm not happy. I'll visit but bring two of my partners, Rahul and Jasmin."

> **Me:** "Great!!!"

The following day the venture trio were seated; visibly uncomfortable and wary. Arms crossed. Bodies stiff. Classic defensive postures as if they expected me to attack them.

By intention I was visibly comfortable and relaxed.

Our quartet reviewed their proposed term sheet paragraph by paragraph.

> **Me:** "Let me share the deal prism Songbird is looking through. We want a *partner*; a relationship among *equals*. Not someone we're reporting to.
>
> "If you purchase a 20% interest, you'll be a meaningful *minority* owner with a single Board seat. *Symmetrical*. Fine.
>
> "What i*sn't* acceptable is your proposed veto power over Board decisions as if you were the *majority* owner.
>
> "*Asymmetrical*. Not fine."

They proposed veto power over high-level, major corporate activities (like selling the business) as well as ground-level operations (we couldn't fire managers without their approval).

They didn't want to be a *partner*. They wanted to be Songbird's *Managing Partner*.

> **Me:** "Given who your fellow Directors are, do you even *want* a control level implying the rest of us are incompetent or irresponsible?
>
> "Should tails wag dogs?"

After a heavily engaged review of *what* the Fund wanted substantively, clarification of *why* they wanted it, and *how* that did (or didn't) make sense given the people and board procedures already in place, everyone was still seated, but now everyone *was* comfortable.

The mutual education forged intellectual and emotional space for the Fund to realize how significantly *this* DealCircle deviated from their normal counterparties, and why their boiler-plate term sheet was "inappropriate-veering-on-offensive."

Why wasn't that surprising?

From a musical perspective, Jerry Garcia illuminated the Dealjammer trap we all fall into:

> *As a musician you fall into certain patterns that you're not conscious of, unless you start listening to yourself on tape a lot. If you do that you start recognizing habits; then you have to try and break them.*

At our end of the telescope we got schooled on why certain provisions were mandatory for regulatory compliance and others under the Fund's confidential limited partnership agreement with their investors.

With all that said, their request for veto power over a sale was *not* mandatory under either. It was a "nice to have" not a "need to have." Normal board approval by an expanded Songbird board would require a bare majority (four out of what would be seven Directors).

If we wanted *them* to think about this *particular* investment (and not their last investment or their next investment), then *we* had to reciprocate. Encyclopedia selling 101.

Thinking it through, we gave weight to the fact that ours was a collegial, collaborative board. If we couldn't get at least five out of the six current Directors to align on a sale, odds were good we shouldn't and wouldn't approve a sale.

The compromise reached was the Fund couldn't veto a sale if a *supermajority* of the newly constituted seven person board (five out of seven Directors) voted in favor. Said differently, no more than one current Director opposed a transaction.

Not customary. Not conventional. Also not unreasonable for a sale, arguably the most important decision in a corporation's lifetime.

Less than what they asked for. More than we wanted to give. A fair trade.

Dealjammers can compromise without feeling compromised.

As they were leaving my home, the following occurred:

Lead Negotiator:	"Marc, before we give you a replacement term sheet we'll call to explain *what* we're trying to accomplish and *why*.
	"You'll let us know if there are impacts on you we hadn't considered and facts we didn't know. Let's avoid more inadvertent tensions."

His guidance was enthusiastically accepted.

If we'd sent the blacklined agreement with our changes back without discussion, we'd have only taken turns *talking*. No one would have been *heard*. That's why **Emails don't create dialogue; they create sequential monologue.**

Author Margaret Millar summarized this phenomenon compactly. "Most conversations are simply monologues delivered in the presence of witnesses."

We needed the opposite: trust-building, *real dialogue*. In physicist David Bohm's words that occurs only "… where two or more people become willing to suspend their certainty in each other's presence."

The deal closed in record time.

A *negotiation* that could have gotten off to a rocky start as a contest of wills shapeshifted into a *discussion* and a fabulous investor working relationship among the Fund, management, and Directors.

Chapter 12 Key Takeaways

- A Dealjammer's mission is to *listen*, and make sure there's no information you're *missin'*. Vocabulary matters. Words matter.

Use age-appropriate, environment-appropriate, and experience-appropriate language. Make it as easy as possible for today's counterparty (today's audience) to hear what you're saying.

There's a different audience for rap, rock, soul, hip hop, Beethoven, jazz, and gospel. There's lots of overlay but also meaningful distinctions. As Jerry Garcia remarked, "If you think of music as a universal language, it still has some very powerful dialects."

- Avoid using technical, financial, or legal terms; they seem unambiguous but are surprisingly susceptible to misunderstanding. They offer what a friend of mine calls a "false sense of precision." Illusory.

Test mutual understanding by using concrete *examples*.

Buyer: "The contract says you'll indemnify us from costs and expenses from 'material' litigation arising from before the Closing. So I'm just wondering, what does 'material' mean? $10,000? $250,000? $1 million? How will I know?"

- Periodically summarize agreements reached *during* a negotiating session as well as *after* a negotiating session.

Later agreements in deals routinely build on earlier negotiating trades. That approach is only sustainable and effective if everyone has the same *cumulative* understanding. Cracks from a small initial fault line can cause an entire structure to come tumbling down.

CHAPTER 13

WHAT COLOR IS THE NEXT SWAN?

When I was nineteen, unusually lucky circumstances found me living and working in Melbourne. Some friends and I visited a zoo exhibit featuring animals unique to Australia. I had read about (but never seen) some of these life forms including koalas (no, they are *not* bears) and platypuses (would you be happier if I said "platypusi"?).

Fascinating but not unexpected.

Then I rounded a corner. The next sight wasn't simply unexpected; it was quite literally shocking.

In the zoos and lagoons of my childhood, all swans were beautiful white birds. Elegant, long-necked, and serene; floating on calm waters.

On this lagoon were elegant, long-necked, and serene *black* birds with distinctive, orange-red beaks. My memories are strong of being totally baffled and thinking "these look exactly like swans, but they can't be. They're *black*."

Massive emotional, intellectual, and cognitive dissonance.

Despite my inability to recognize them, these *were* black swans (indigenous to Australia and New Zealand, known to European explorers since 1697, but still largely unknown elsewhere).

What you perceive has to make sense to your brain, not just your eyes, to retain as useful visual information.

My takeaway was not that the universe unexpectedly consists solely of white or black swans. My takeaway was that *not all swans are white*.

Three-valued logic. Not two-valued logic. Vastly different. The "opposite" of white isn't "black." The opposite of white is *not* white. Enormously more expansive universe.

The epiphany was that with more experience or education, black swans would have been within my field of vision, so not unexpected.

Unlike unicorns, black swans are real.

My physical-world black swan encounter occurred decades before author-statistician Nassim Nicholas Taleb (*The Black Swan: The impact of the Highly Improbable*) popularized the valuable black swan metaphor into mainstream thinking. Like any great metaphor it's useful if not taken farther than sensible.

At the risk of gross oversimplification:

- *White* swan events are regularly occurring, predictable elements of a system and should be expected,

- *Gray* swan events aren't common but they're not improbable or unknown, and

- *Black* swan events are invisible and totally unpredictable, and if a black swan event occurs it has a colossal impact.

Deals and documents brim with swans of many hues. Some predicaments are *predictable* (white or gray swans) and others *unpredictable* (black swans). Some merely have a "Touch of Grey."

Some deal-killing, negative circumstances and provisions are *self-created* by a counterparty while others are *externally* created. Possibilities and permutations are infinite.

Do Dealjammers have to be so smart they can foresee and plan for everything?

SPOILER ALERT: Relax. No one is that smart. Life isn't perfect.

Deals, negotiations, people, and life are messy. (I'm sorry I didn't figure that out sooner.)

As physicist/philosopher Niels Bohr (not Yogi Berra or Casey Stengel) noted, "Prediction is very difficult, especially if it's about the future."

With enough deal data and experience, some impediments are predictable enough you can foresee their *possibility,* even if you aren't sure they are *inevitable.* Pattern recognition lets you spotlight them. Forewarned you can protect yourself better.

But what of the impossible-to-predict but inevitable black swan?

Your best protection is creating flexible deals (and documents) facilitating fast, improvised responses when black swans inevitably emerge.

Maximize your optionalities.

As blues guitarist John Mayall says, leave yourself "room to move."

Back to encyclopedia ground-zero selling principles.

A major goal is reducing (to the irreducible minimum) the number of people needing to say "yes" before you can leave the house with a signed check. Eliminate anyone's opportunity to say "no" and block your sale.

Intuitively the fewer people who have to consent within the first two circles of the DealCircle (Buyer, Seller, attorneys, accountants, and deal advisors) the more probable, easier, and faster your agreement will be implemented.

What about DealCirclers in the third and fourth circles? Their interests may be tangential but their consent and cooperation still needed. Landlords. EPA. Almost-invisible, potentially random deal killers.

These are *white* swans, not *black* swans. Establish a reasonable critical path (with substantial margin for error) to obtain what the deal needs from them consistent with the deal schedule.

Tactics that are effective with the counterparties in the first and second circles (people who usually have cash on the line), can't be applied to the third and fourth. They don't have a dog in your fight and so aren't susceptible to Urgency Accelerators. Without a dog third and fourth DealCircler's don't lose anything if the deal doesn't close.

With that conceptual introduction to the wide world of deal swans behind us, let's see if we can systematically de-risk the future.

A startup running out of cash is clearly a *white* swan

We've already seen that the consistent startup and early-stage experience is that everything takes at least twice as long (and costs three times as much) as your most conservative cash projection.

That's the norm not the exception. Ask anyone who has done more than one startup if sales and cash happened faster or slower than projected.

Founder and CEO of OfficeMax, Bob Hurwitz, was a sophisticated and experienced executive and operator who had run successful businesses. That said, he and I were newbies at financing fast-paced startups, companies universally requiring multiple rounds of equity raises to support growth.

Most Sunday evenings from Fourth of July weekend 1987 through the balance of the year was Groundhog Day (Groundhog Night?). Sitting at my small, round, wooden kitchen table writing and revising OfficeMax's Business Plan with Bob.

Highly capable accountants set up detailed cash projections. They reflected capital consumption consistent with the anticipated growth rate for a regional superstore chain planning to open dozens of physical locations.

Because Bob was older than me (not to mention the client!), I (almost) always deferred to his business judgment when our views differed.

As everything was being finalized to start raising the first round of outside capital (Convertible Preferred Stock), we focused on the official "charter documents" governing the company, its Directors, and stockholders. These were mainstream, dense, plain vanilla documents written in incomprehensible "legalese" (technical jargon). I was translating them into human English so Bob could confirm they satisfied his major business objectives:

- $3 million of Preferred Stock existed to sell to investors,
- in a sale of the business, investors would get their money back first before Common Stockholders, and
- Bob's Common Stock *totally* controlled electing Directors or approving sale of the business.

Good priorities.

After doing that, I volunteered:

> **Me to Bob:** "Just FYI, the documents include Blank Check Preferred Stock."

That's what startup lawyers characterize as routine provisions. The result is roughly analogous to your signing an otherwise blank check and giving it to someone. You've implicitly given them permission to fill in the balance of the check, including who gets paid and in what amount. Personally, I don't trust anyone that much.

Similarly, blank check stock like this doesn't have any fixed financial characteristics established at the outset. The security has been *authorized* by the stockholders *now* for *sale* by the company in the *future*.

When later on the Directors know exactly what they want the terms of a particular preferred stock to be, they can establish specific rights (liquidation preference, dividends, voting rights, etc.) for new preferred stock without needing further stockholder approval.

Super-fast. Super flexible.

CEO Bob to me: "We don't need blank check preferred. $3 million from this Preferred Stock is all the money we'll ever need and the only security we'll ever sell.

"If investors read this clause they'll get confused and think we're going to raise more money or trick them.

"Confused people say 'no.' Confused people don't buy stock. Don't over-lawyer this!"

Hmmmmmm. I must not have explained this concept very well!

Maybe it would have gone better if I'd led with the important comment that in the early-stage world *operational speed* is a *tactic*, operational speed is a *strategy*, and operational speed is a competitive *barrier*.

The corporate finance corollary is that *flexibility* is a *tactic*, flexibility is a *strategy*, and flexibility is a *competitive barrier*.

Blank check provisions are the poster child for financial flexibility. If we didn't need them later on, then we didn't need them. So be it.

But if we *did* need them later on (and we didn't have them) that would be a humongous problem.

We'd have to negotiate terms of the to-be-issued-and-sold *Series B* Preferred Stock with our current preferred stock investors. We'd need their approval before creating documents to start selling. Otherwise, we'd take the risk of negotiating terms with a Series B investor and then having to revert to our current investors for their approval. What would we do if existing investors didn't approve them?

The unaffordably expensive (and possibly fatal) cost would be extending the time required to execute a Series B round. Speed to close and take in cash would be impaired.

Bad tactics. Bad strategy.

Properly admonished by Bob and appropriately abashed, I went slightly rogue and included the blank check language.

It wasn't rap artist Paris's "Devil Made Me Do It"; not even the Grateful Dead's "Friend of the Devil." It was recalling financial advisor Howard Ruff's perceptive comment that "It wasn't raining when Noah built the ark."

Startups are time, cash, and emotion vampires.

A few months after our initial preferred stock round closed, the world had dramatically changed. Our carefully crafted, newly minted business plan was already inadequate and outdated.

Competition was intensifying. Being a regional office supply superstore wasn't sufficient.

To succeed we had to become a *national* retailer capable of competing with the financial strength and rapidly accelerating growth rate of major competitors like Staples and Office Depot. It had become a race for space.

Opening and stocking inventory for hundreds of stores required obtaining equipment and people plus immeasurably more money than mere dozens. Right now.

Bob phoned on a Friday morning asking what pieces of paper were required to raise more money. Intending to tease him, I responded,

> **Me to Bob:** "Without blank check preferred, the legally required steps to raise Series B Preferred are:
>
> - amend the charter documents,
> - circulate a detailed proxy/ information statement to all existing Convertible Preferred stockholders, and
> - get affirmative votes from them.
>
> "With luck, six weeks from start to finish."

Bob (in evi- dent frustration and despair):	"We don't have that much time. Today is Friday. I have to be getting investor com-mitments this weekend."

Recognizing his pain, I stopped yanking his chain.

Me:	"Don't worry; it's going to be all right."

Bob:	"Didn't you hear *anything* I said? If we can't raise money for six weeks we're dead. Game over."

Me:	"Then I have good news. I *completely* ig-nored your instructions. We *do* have blank check preferred. All you need is a Board vote approving terms of a new Series B Preferred Stock. We'll do that *today*. You can start selling *tomorrow*."

A sudden need for more capital than planned routinely occurs to countless startups.

It's perverse. You need more capital because the business is *under*-performing and eating cash. You need more capital because the business is *over*performing, doing better than expected, so expansion capital is necessary long before anticipated.

From my perspective this capital crunch was a white swan; not even gray and absolutely *not* black. This crisis was possible-to-probable even if not inevitable.

Armed with the ability to raise capital (a bona fide security) Bob did so almost immediately. Series B cash was in the corporate bank account about a week later.

Creating speed and flexibility around maintaining cash adequacy didn't guarantee success but it opened the potential for triumph.

Cash is a proxy for time; time is a proxy for opportunity.

It cost the company nothing to reserve a supply of highly adaptable blank check stock. Three paragraphs were added to the twelve-page Certificate of Incorporation.

Those few words positioned the company to maneuver in a crisis (or to avoid a crisis). Corporate swans of any hue (internal or external) could be responded to without negotiation and with no loss of time or money.

All reward. No risk. The best conceivable risk-reward ratio.

As we've observed before, *The most successful negotiation is the one you never need to have.*

A change-of-control provision in a lease is a less obvious (but clearly) *white* swan

If you've accepted money to launch a new business from investors (other than your in-laws), the implicit understanding is you'll grow the business and then sell it (or otherwise create liquidity for investors). An exit of some type is presumed even if not articulated.

Every startup businessperson is under intense pressure to quickly enter into first time arrangements and accelerate the business. Employment agreements, stock option plans and grants, distribution contracts, and (in this case) shopping center leases.

It's super hard emotionally to think about what's involved in *selling* your business when you're totally engaged in *starting* and growing your business. Almost bad karma.

In that environment, it's quintessentially human to focus on getting something signed today, rather than spending lots of time worrying about issues that won't have a corporate impact for months or years. Tomorrow will take care of itself.

But time passes quickly. In political commentator George Will's words, the "future has a way of arriving unannounced." Those early arrangements made in haste can have pernicious effects later on.

I admired Bob's deliberate process of thinking through the key clauses in his financing documents. It's easy to be overwhelmed with wholesale pieces of paper without focusing on the handful of issues that can single-handedly prevent you from critical actions.

For lack of more graceful vocabulary, I think of those as "choke points"; particularly those getting in the way of raising capital or liquidity events like selling the business.

Included in the "friends and family" financing were some nationally prominent shopping center owners with highly desirable retail sites. The company would inevitably want to lease space and open stores at some of them. Those lease terms could either facilitate or cripple future corporate financings (debt or equity) as well as liquidity events.

Even with $3 million of cash, we were not an immediately magnetic tenant. No branded name. No track record of success. Any landlord entering into a lease arrangement with us was taking a meaningful chance.

The strength of our dreams significantly exceeded the strength of our balance sheet.

Based primarily on their immense respect for Bob, a friendly investor offered an extraordinary retail location, favorable economic terms, and their standard lease form (including a "change-of-control" clause).

For understandable reasons landlords like to know who they're dealing with and whose credit they're relying on. A common protective mechanism is a landlord's right to terminate a lease if the tenant's ownership (or sometimes management) changes without landlord's consent (i.e., a "change-of-control"). That's precisely what would happen if/when we sold the company.

Given that reality, an appropriate response from us would have been to immediately say, "thank you," and sign the ten-year lease before our "Investor-Landlord" could change their minds.

What caused a slight negotiating detour was knowing that this arrangement was only step one in launching, growing, and subsequently selling the company.

If all went well, this first lease could be precedent-setting, creating a standard foundational document we could use for all subsequent landlord negotiations.

If you put your head in the lion's mouth enough times, eventually the lion wins.

Based on our expansion plans, if every lease had a change-of-control provision, selling the company might require obtaining written consents from dozens (if not hundreds) of landlords.

Practical pitfalls and adverse economic consequences were clear from my prior experience when landlords had that much leverage over retail chains.

- *Worst* case: we'd be reaching out to unmotivated people (landlords who gained nothing from a transaction) and find they were *unavailable* or *unwilling* to consent.

- *Best* case: they were responsive and *willing* to consent but only on re-negotiated terms benefitting them (rent increases, longer fixed lease term commitments, or more costs paid by tenant). Lions know when to pounce.

We were a corporate pipsqueak. Negotiating power and leverage invariably favored Landlord.

That said, our foresight about the negative consequences of this provision gave us resolute staying power. We wanted to stop hundreds of time-consuming, expensive landlord negotiations before they started.

At a minimum those negotiations would cost us time and money, factors which could significantly, adversely impact the value we'd receive at exit.

We shared that immodest vision with Landlord, and opined that whether in his Landlord Hat or Investor Hat our mutual interests were best served by removing this otherwise non-negotiable, standard clause.

Me to Landlord: "You think we're on opposite sides of this provision. In your *Landlord* Hat you want control over who you're doing business with. Fair enough. In your *Investor* Hat you should *beg us* to remove the clause; not simply *let us* remove the clause."

Landlord: "Are you crazy? Why would I do that?"

Me: "You'll make more money investing with us than landlording us. Buyers with the financial capability to buy this company will have better credit than we do, and probably be a better tenant for you.

"If you retain this change-of-control right, you're knowingly putting our company at the mercy of all our *other* future landlords and diminishing value for your Investor Hat.

"Why would you do that"?

Landlord: "That's painful but persuasive logic. We'll take it out. Marc, don't make me regret this!"

Could we have signed the lease as presented, said "thank you," and dealt with comparable provisions only when it was an actual problem at sale? Sure. But why give anyone (let alone *hundreds* of people you don't know) the opportunity to hold you captive for time or money at your exit, the liquidity event which is the most critical moment in a corporation's life?

Blanche DuBois to the contrary, one "cannot count on the kindness of strangers." I try not to.

Our Landlord was the industry's gold standard. He knew us. We knew him. If he removed the clause, so would all others.

Surprisingly small, easy-to-overlook, almost unnoticed negotiations at the beginning (and end) of deals can dramatically impact operational corporate value created over many years.

Blank check preferred stock was the first. Eliminating change-of-control provisions was the second.

I'd rather own some percentage of something than 100% of nothing, or a Tyranny of One

This Maxim's universal wisdom seemed unassailable until miserable experience as a Director/investor made brutally clear it isn't.

A highflying company easily raised $500 million from 2004 through 2007 in eight separate rounds of Preferred Stock (Series A through Series H), each at a higher valuation than the prior round. (It's always easier to raise money when you don't need it.)

Then brutal capital marketplace changes impacted us (and all others) during the 2008 worldwide financial crisis.

Now we desperately needed capital. After months of effort not a penny could be obtained from existing or new investors. All were busy protecting their other portfolio companies.

Reducing our *pre*-money valuation asking price dramatically below the most recent *post*-money valuations didn't stir any interest.

Corporate existentialism (company life or death) made it clear that **What matters about capital isn't price, it's availability.**

With cash dwindling hourly, corporate survival was possible only by accepting a vulture-like funding alternative, a valuation nearly 95% lower than the most recent Series H Preferred Stock sale.

To all intents and purposes, 100% of the money invested by existing stockholders would be wiped out.

CEO to Board: "They're offering $5 million to buy 95% of the company; a Series I Preferred Stock with a triple liquidation preference. Our current stockholders would only own 5%.

"The *good* news is they'd hire most of our employees."

Board (unan-	*"Ludicrous!* Reject this offer out-of-hand. It's
imously	not just *ugly*, it's *punitive.*"
and angrily):	

CEO to Board:	"With due respect, when a single offer is your only choice, by default it *is* attractive.
	"Of course, as always, I remain responsive to your wise guidance and suggestions. Who do *you* think we should get the money from?"

Best case, this offer could be viewed as a cramdown recapitalization. It would be a harsh, formal restructuring of the company's existing Common Stock and Preferred Stock. All stock and our stockholders would be subjugated to the new, vastly superior rights and ownership of the new investors.

Current investors could conceivably recover a miniscule percentage of their invested capital, but only if the company performed extraordinarily well on a go-forward basis.

With more than 200 stockholders (institutions as well as high net worth individuals and family offices), implementing this massive reshuffling in weeks would be a logistical nightmare under the best of circumstances.

This *wasn't* the best of circumstances.

Separate consents (positive votes) were needed from investors holding a majority in *each* of the eight series of outstanding Preferred Stock.

Analysis showed only one stockholder could single-handedly block the deal. He owned a majority of stock in the smallest financing round.

Management knew the stockholder well and reached out.

Management:	"Here are the ugly details and financial consequences. Before talking with any other stockholders, we wanted to inform you directly and make sure you'll vote in favor."

Lone Ranger	"Disappointing, but I'm a big boy. Lucky
Stockholder	for me I'll still be worth $1 billion."
(not happily but	
without any ap-	
parent anger):	

| **Management:** | "Thanks (?) for your vote of confidence. |
| | "Now we'll tackle the complex paperwork to get approval from the other seven rounds of Preferred Stock. Documents will be sent to you and your lawyer by week's end." |

Voluminous documents were prepared; proxy statements disclosing all operating and financial facts, background, and consequences of the restructuring. Detailed explanatory letters and proxies were sent to all stockholders, phone calls made, and cats herded.

Directors met at least weekly, and sometimes daily.

Amid the hubbub, management checked in sporadically with the Lone Ranger Stockholder about the status of his proxy. Each time he apologized for delays in returning it.

Sometimes the time lag was caused by "too much work," and sometimes by "too much vacation." Regardless of the proffered justification, he always pleasantly reiterated he would return his documentation "soon."

We focused on stockholders whose permission we *didn't* have and obtained their approvals and proxies.

The day before the deal was Closing (with papers not yet returned), I met with Lone Ranger Stockholder's investment advisor.

Lone Ranger	"Marc, my client demands a different
Stockholder's	structure giving him economic and voting
investment	rights more favorable to him than any oth-
advisor:	er current stockholder."

Me:	"You're kidding me, right?
	"Those changes would void the votes and proxies we already have. New Board approval would be needed before starting a second time to obtain stockholder approval.
	"Even if Directors wanted to accommodate him, this demand can't physically be met in time to close tomorrow which is our last day of cash runway.
	"In four words, it's *im pos sib le.*"
Lone Ranger Stockholder's investment advisor:	"I'm not a lawyer, and even I knew that. Almost word-for-word what I unsuccessfully told my client yesterday. It *didn't* change his mind.
	"I'll try again, but you should proceed as if he *won't* change his mind."

Despite the difficulty of predicting the future he correctly anticipated his client's negative response.

Our lawyers advised us to shut the company down and have all Directors resign the next day. We did. I did.

The incredibly positive outcome he single-handedly engineered?

No Stockholder would receive *any* compensation for their stock. *Everyone* (including the unexpected dissident) would receive *nothing*.

Emotion and ego can trump raw economics. What's irrational from your point of view may not be irrational seen through the other end of a telescope.

It didn't help us any, but we tried imagining what prompted this passive-aggressive, seemingly irrational behavior. Our speculation was the decision may have been rational from his perspective but not reasonable from anyone else's.

Lone Ranger   "If *I* have so little upside from the re-
Stockholder   structured deal,

(hypothetically   "I'd just as soon be done with the whole
to himself):   thing and take my tax loss, *plus*

"As a bonus *I* can hurt some people *I'm* mad at.

"Bury the company and *I* will move on. But most importantly, *I'm* still worth $1 billion."

There's no "I" in team. His outrageous behavior resulted in a stunningly adverse impact to all others.

He may (or may not) have accomplished something that made *him* feel good (perhaps rational behavior?) but commercially unreasonable.

What would have been rational from our perspective (even if unwelcomed) is if he had forthrightly mustered his veto power when we initially approached him.

We knew and acknowledged his vote was the lynchpin to a deal. At that moment, he could have demanded concessions. More likely than not, we'd have granted them; giving him a possibility (however small) of economic gain.

When this sequence occurred his behavior seemed more petulant and childish than anything else. Why ask for something that you absolutely know cannot occur?

In retrospect there are some alternative theories which would have made me more cautious in my counterparty behavioral analysis.

People derive pleasure from having and exercising power. (I'd offer you some examples, but all you need to do is read the first page of any newspaper.) What could be more powerful than stopping a transaction hundreds of other people wanted to occur?

It's also possible that the relatively few (and in fairness highly speculative) dollars of upside to him (which to *me* was "something"), may have been "nothing" to a billionaire. Such a small sum that he wouldn't stop to pick it up if he tripped over it on the street.

Do you still stop to collect pennies? Nickels? Dimes? Quarters? Most people have a cutoff threshold.

Until a deal closes, someone with veto power may use it as leverage to extract a concession. Never underestimate that rational as well as irrational people can and do cut off their noses to spite their face (and *yours*).

If you volunteer to be a hostage, prepare to pay ransom.

Unintentionally (and embarrassingly) we had put ourselves in position to be extorted. We had accidentally given a stockholder with miniscule ownership the ability to thwart the majority and demand ransom.

If you put your head in the mouths of enough lions, enough times, the lions win.

The Lone Ranger Stockholder's specific bad behavior wasn't specifically foreseeable.

What *was* foreseeable is that other investors armed with the same power, in the same circumstances, would similarly have demanded something in return for surrendering it.

Permitted enough times, *Possible* becomes *Probable* and *Inevitable*.

If you agree it's a good idea to stay out of the mouths of deal lions (as well as avoiding being a deal hostage), here's a thought to ponder. Except under pain of death (no matter how much you trust them) never give *anyone* an explicit or implicit veto power.

In my Dad-speak, "trust your Mother, but cut the cards."

This tip isn't likely to make you laugh, but it may save you some tears.

Swans come in many hues

You won't see what you aren't looking for. (You may not even see what you *are* looking for.) Your *black* swan may be my *white* swan. And there are at least 50 shades of gray.

On to the next dramas and some specific tactics from the art of auctions (not the auctions of art).

Chapter 13 Key Takeaways

- The world is complex, and black swan events occur. No planning exercise, financial projection, or set of documents can (or should) anticipate every possible contingency. Negotiating is a game of realistically grappling with statistical probability.

Pattern recognition from learning and experience lets Dealjammers focus on the issues *most likely* to occur or impact them operationally or financially.

Ignore less-than-one percenters. Get the big ones right. Life and deals can't be made risk-free.

- That said, ***the most successful negotiation is the one you never need to have*** because you planned around it.

Resist any provision that impedes raising money (*absence* of blank check preferred) or selling the business (*presence* of change-of-control provisions).

No single problematical clause is inevitably fatal, but each decreases odds of success by giving outside parties (like landlords or lenders) leverage at excruciatingly sensitive moments in a company's lifetime.

Probability says if you need cooperation from others enough times, sometimes you *won't* get it. You've made yourself a hostage. Why would you be surprised when someone demands ransom?

Common sense says even if you get the cooperation or consents you need, you'll pay a cost in time, money, or both.

Those are bad bets. ***If you put your head in the lion's mouth enough times, eventually the lion wins.***

CHAPTER 14

NEGOTIATING IS THEATER WITH CONSEQUENCES AND RESULTS

As the Monty Python troupe used to say, "And now for something completely different."

Our storytelling has already helicoptered into private acquisition negotiations between two counterparties as well as an *informal* auction involving unlimited counterparties.

What's left to explore is my favorite sell side process: a well-orchestrated and well-attended *formal* sales auction. It's the consummate use of time, fear, greed, and leverage.

Auction deadlines are simultaneously real as well as artificial. Universe of buyers is fixed. Time allotted for bidding/negotiating is compressed and rigid. Assuming the minimum bid price is cleared, there'll be only a single winner and many losers.

Dealmaking theater at its most robust. Room and opportunity for creative Dealjamming combined with rigorous critical path planning.

Corporate auctions star rivals in unrivalled deal theater

The best corporate auction from Seller's perspective has at least two financially capable parties bidding, preferably antagonistic competitors.

Each wants to win. Only one can. Neither wants to lose. One will. Scarcity.

Engaged bidders (for businesses or homes) routinely,

- get trapped in the exacerbated emotion of an auction moment,
- extend themselves financially well beyond what they intended, and
- later wonder what zombie took over their body and made that bid?

Formal corporate auctions are complex games utilizing many now-familiar-to-you skills and tactics:

- Time pressure.
- Scarcity.
- Competition.
- Fear of missing out.

The process intrinsically brings about and unleashes value.

By design and definition the auction opportunity is scarce (you can only buy the same company once).

My introductory experience with frenzied formal auctions wasn't corporate, and it wasn't the Grateful Dead, but it *was* about music-focused corporations.

While meeting in New York with an industry heavyweight, something cropped up just as our chat was ending, keeping her unhappily confined to her office for the evening.

The serendipitous result was a last-minute gift to me of her highly sought-after, reserved seat tickets to the 2004 Crossroads Guitar Auction at Christie's. Row 4. Directly in front of the auctioneer.

The charity auction featured stellar instruments owned by Eric Clapton, or donated by his friends like Stevie Ray Vaughan and J.J. Cale.

Rock royalty and musical legends redefining glitter.

Hundreds of well-heeled, impeccably dressed patrons were flanked by lengthy rows of individually staffed telephone banks, so global bidders could participate through their telephone avatars.

Bidding was robust. Items sold quickly well above their pre-auction estimated price ranges.

The pièce de résistance unfolded like this.

Auctioneer:	"And last but not least, we'll be selling 'Blackie,' Eric Clapton's guitar for 30 years. "Can I get an opening bid of $50,000?"
#1 Bidder:	$100,000
#2 Bidder:	$1*10*,000
#1 Bidder:	$1*20*,000
#3 Bidder (Guitar Center):	*$500,000*

Astounded crowd. Murmurs swept through every row of the enormous hall.

#4 Bidder (House of Blues):	$600,000
Guitar Center:	*$700,000*
House of Blues:	$800,000
Guitar Center (*decisively*):	$8*50*,000
Auctioneer:	"Are there any advances? No? Last lot of the evening. "*Sold* for $850,000."

A 60-second master class in Dealjamming. No way to know if their tactics and strategies were spontaneous or scripted. Either way it was brilliant.

The first three bids were conventional: an opening bid above the asking price, followed closely by comparatively modest incremental increases of $10,000 (10%). The crowd wasn't sleeping through these exchanges, but neither were they electrified.

Guitar Center's initial bid galvanized the party.

As an outsider there's no way to know what analysis led them to a single supersize step from $120,000 to $500,000. It's not obvious how they would they have characterized their methodology.

Quadrupling their previous bid? Increasing the price by almost $400,000? *Not* a modest incremental increase. Either gambit strikingly distinguished them from other bidders.

Breath-taking. Jaw-dropping. A bodacious deal spiel.

Guitar Center didn't simply *break* the developing rhythmic bidding pattern; they *shattered* it. Only their fiercest, most deep-pocketed competitor (House of Blues) remained in the fray with little time to alter their own strategy.

This bold tactic was the opposite of deal creep. It was deal *leap*. Instantaneously narrowing a mega-size bidding funnel from dozens to two. Guitar Center magnified the already built-in auction time pressure and instantly intensified it for House of Blues.

What an educational moment. A lesson for the ages.

"One More Saturday Night"

When there's nothing to lose, you can't lose anything.

A few years after the Christie experience, my wife and I were at a Saturday night charity auction dinner in San Francisco.

Among the featured items was a guitar autographed by the Grateful Dead's rhythm guitarist (Bob Weir). Among other gems he penned one of my favorite tunes, "One More Saturday Night."

The instrument was gorgeous, inducing in me (and others) what musicians refer to as "gear" lust. An "American Beauty."

There's no way I could resist bidding ... until it occurred to me that I'm a piano player. What good was a guitar to me?

Not wanting to waste opportunity I called a plausible buyer, an East Coast friend (and frequent Grateful Dead concert companion). He was reached at what sounded like a raucous, late night party in his neighborhood.

> **Me** (excitedly): "It's a Gibson Les Paul standard with a flame-maple top and sunburst finish."

> **Friend:** "That charity does great work, so I'd be delighted to bid up to $5,000. But, Marc, that's it. I'm not willing to pay any more than $5,000."

He authorized me to bid on his behalf.

The guitar's provenance and aesthetics would make for a hot item. Many would bid for it, particularly for a "worthy cause." (Translation? Tax-deductible.)

Post-phone call/pre-auction images of the Clapton auction appeared. How to apply those observed-if-not-yet-applied lessons in this dramatically lower-key event?

Critical deal considerations:

- *scarce asset* (arguably one-of-a-kind),
- absolute *dollar limit* ($5,000),
- *fixed timeframe* (auction ended in an hour), and
- *DealCirclers visible.* (Except for me, no Clapton-type telephone bidders to contend with.)

My recollection was strong about how Guitar Center's hyper-aggressive tactics and instantaneous responses to other bids had:

- discouraged others,
- rapidly reduced bidders to the super-serious, and
- let Guitar Center quickly emerge as the winner, the final bidder.

The best possible storyline for purchasing Weir's guitar (bidding sequence, tone, timing, and rhythm) was similarly designed to demonstrate unquenchable resolve albeit on a dramatically smaller scale. Casual bidders would find an accelerating pace off-putting and drop out.

The message? "I" would not be outbid.

Auctioneer:	"Can I get an opening bid of $100?"
#1 Bidder:	"Yes."
Me (with no pause):	"$1,000."
#2 Bidder:	"$1,100; I increase by *$100.*"
Me (with no pause):	$2,000."
#2 Bidder:	"$2,300; I increase by *$300.*"
Me (with no pause):	"$3,000."
#2 Bidder:	"$3,200; I increase by *$200.*"
Me (with no pause):	"$4,000."
#2 Bidder:	"$4,200; I increase by *$200.*"
Me (with no pause):	"$5,000."

It might look as if with extreme bidding increases I was negotiating against myself. My sense however was that mere incremental bids ($100, $200, or $300 like the #2 bidder) would have encouraged others to remain engaged and escalate the final price. Not my objective.

Common sense and moderation get easily suspended in an auction, so there was a palpable danger to that approach. No one would have felt sufficiently threatened to drop out of the process.

With no more of my friend's money to bid, it was now or never. No decision-maker available to appeal to. End of the line.

My tactics may have been sound. (Pun intended.) The other bidder may have run out of money. My friend may have just gotten lucky. Regardless he bought the guitar for $5,000.

Boiling Frog

The following analogy about incremental steps is not guaranteed to be scientifically accurate but may still be helpful.

I have no idea *why* you'd do the following, but if you put a frog in a pot in *hot* (but not boiling) water, on a stove (showers are 100 degrees), and slowly, slowly, slowly turn the heat up one or two degrees at a time (incrementally) until the water is boiling (212 degrees), the frog stays and eventually boils to death.

Incredibly *sad* news.

By contrast, if you throw a frog directly into a pot of *boiling* water, the frog immediately hops out and survives. Amphibian response and tactics change because the contrast between air temperature and boiling water is vivid and compelling. The opposite of incremental.

Incredibly *good* news.

Bidding increases of $100 are incremental. The equivalent of two degrees of temperature. The bidders keep on bidding.

Bidding increases of $1,000 *aren't* incremental. They attract attention. The equivalent of 212 degrees, a magnitude more than $100. As close to pouring boiling water on the other bidders as I could.

All but one immediately jumped out and even she bolted out of the auction pot after five bids.

Funnel Negotiations

Sales funnels are used routinely in business. The company records all customers they have contacted or (intend to contact), identifies selling steps (first contact, meeting, document exchange, legal approval, and procurement approval), and tracks progress being made on each.

That's the widest possible funnel list to analyze expected customer sales. The probability of making a sale increases as each additional step is checked off, helping the business focus.

Less-likely sales (where the customer's steps haven't advanced as expected) drop off or are dropped off. The funnel is wide but partly random in the beginning, and narrower (but more focused) at the end.

"Negotiation funnels" are the analogous term I coined for corporate auctions.

Initially Sellers want a relatively broad range of participants in the negotiation funnel to test the market and maximize price discovery and interest. The scope of the outreach is established.

- Private equity funds? *Yes.*
- Venture capital funds? *No.*
- Strategic acquirors? *Yes.*

With "bulk" achieved (quantity more than quality), interested parties can be played off against each other and winnowed over time. As identified bidders drop out, Seller can widen or narrow the funnel criteria as the capable are distinguished from the *incapable*.

Maximize your optionalities.

Impala's Family Advisor employed similar negotiation funnel tactics in her *informal* auction process of the family-owned financially distressed business. Roughly the same strategy was used in *formal* auction processes by Christie's auctioneer as well as the Bob Weir Charity Auction.

What happens if you mix wisdom derived from Clapton's auction with the Grateful Dead's "American Beauty"?

What's generally true is rarely universally true.

Dealjamming starts well before Seller prepares for a sale, retains an intermediary, or establishes the size, scope, flavor, and criteria for bidders to be invited to a formal auction.

Here's a sense of the time, place, and players.

The industry was effectively an actively acquisitive duopoly. Goliath #1 and Goliath #2 had a combined 80% national market share.

As super competent strategic buyers, each had made many "tuck-in" acquisitions (i.e., buying small competitors and folding them into their existing national operations). Each had demonstrated experience in fast-moving deals and had ample cash on their balance sheets.

Ideal bidders.

Triad Unlimited was the next largest business in the industry. No smaller industry competitors had financial ability to purchase us. We could acquire them as tuck-ins, but not the other way around.

Despite great management and operators, Triad couldn't ever catch the two leaders through organic growth or even frenzied smaller acquisitions. The delta was realistically insurmountable.

Reluctantly we concluded our best strategic plan for creating stockholder value would be to sell to either Goliath #1 or #2 and present ourselves as the only remaining significant asset on the playing table.

Let one of them (and by definition, *only* one of them) meaningfully advance their size, prospects, profitability, and competitive position relative to the other by buying us.

More expensive for them than ten tuck-ins but still a bargain.

We retained a deal intermediary well-known in the industry with an unusually restrictive mandate: talk with Goliath #1 and Goliath #2 and no one else. Don't deviate from the blunt, straightforward message we have painstakingly framed.

Why?

Triad's value was greater to either industry Goliath than any other possible buyer, including non-strategic financial buyers or private equity funds looking for a platform acquisition.

Of equal tactical relevance was that the Goliaths had gone head-to-head multiple times and were unconcealed fierce enemies. Neither was a gracious or happy loser. (Fabulous!)

We intended a tightly choreographed corporate "Party for Two." (Apologies to Shania Twain.) What we didn't want was a widespread auction to every conceivable bidder. No Impala redux with its slow-moving, informal auction reaching out to even the most remotely possible buyers.

Our first negotiation in this deal was with our intermediary. She asked for a standard investment banking fee as if she were running a full, time-consuming auction.

Good for her. Exactly what *she* should have done. If she hadn't, we wouldn't have hired her.

We appreciated her moxie (but declined the opportunity) and let her know this would be the easiest, most certain paycheck she would ever get. The deal equivalent of shooting fish in a barrel.

Good for us. Exactly what *we* should have done.

The probability of her making a sale to one of the Goliaths seemed all but certain. Without that shared belief she wouldn't be the intermediary we should work with. She might also contemplate finding another line of work.

Our offer of a much smaller fixed fee was accepted. (Parenthetically if we didn't win this negotiation, *we* also should try to obtain gainful employment elsewhere.)

This was the detailed, highly crafted, message she delivered on our behalf:

Intermediary (to each Industry Goliath's CEO):	"You know me. I'm a straight shooter. "I'm working with Triad Unlimited. They're serious about selling and at the right price will sell."

Knowing both Goliaths very well, we also encouraged her to share that she wasn't born yesterday, and she wasn't going to provide price guidance. The sales/negotiating pitch was that this was the ultimate one-of-a-kind asset, the epitome of priceless.

Who could begin to place a fixed value on such a precious gem?

Intermediary:	"I'm only talking with you and your biggest competitor. You know who. "You both understand this industry intimately and are familiar with Seller's operations and locations. Neither of you needs time for diligence. The financial statements we're providing tell the whole story. "This is Thursday. We place a premium on speed."

The "message-speech" was designed to be melodramatic; so guileless (and true) as to be immediately believable.

Intermediary:	"The standard purchase price multiple in the industry is 15 times trailing 12-month revenues for mere tuck-ins. "My client is the most meaningful private company left to buy and should be valued accordingly. Triad represents 40% of all the industry revenue players left to be consolidated. "Whoever acquires them gets an immediate boost in their public stock price and in market share operationally."

That said, we didn't want to totally foreclose the possibility of one Goliath putting forth an enormous offer to stop the auction before it started.

Intermediary: "If you want to make a preemptive offer, feel free."

Each competitor: "What does *preemptive* mean"?

Intermediary: "A bid so high you'll be embarrassed you're making it. A bid so high it will top any other conceivable bid. And we have vivid imaginations.

"We're also big believers in the Seller's Mantra. Air-tight confidentiality provisions are contained in the Non-Disclosure Agreement you'll sign.

"As to the all-important element of *certainty* you'll need to back up any offer with:

- *no* financing contingencies,
- *no* board approval, and
- *minimal* diligence."

Dealing from a luxurious position of strength she played her cards with zest.

Intermediary: "You know where to reach me. Do *not* contact them directly.

"By the way, if Triad doesn't sell now, they're going public next year and raising big bucks. They'll pursue acquisitions aggressively, removing many of your natural tuck-ins.

"If that happens, my hunch is that *you* (or your competitor) will eventually purchase

> Seller 'further on down the road.' By then they'll be much bigger and more desirable, and purchase price will reflect that.
>
> "Like the ads trying to sell you oil filters for your car say, you can pay me *now* or you can pay me *later*."

From late Friday *afternoon* until late Friday *night* our intermediary talked non-stop with both competitors. In between calls she talked with our CEO and me until midnight.

Our questions were endless.

- *Who* was on the phone for each buyer? CEO? CFO? Others?
- *What* was their tone of voice, level of commitment, and resolve to do a deal?
- *Where* were they calling from, and *when* and *where* did they propose meeting?
- *How* did they propose proceeding? In person or via conference call?

Even the most trivial detail can yield critical information.

It turned out that all calls were between our intermediary and Goliath's respective CEOs. Both executives were calling from home on a weekend night.

A specific reason we reached out to them on a Thursday (i.e., not Monday, Tuesday, or Wednesday) was precisely to obtain those kinds of deal insights. Their rapid response, willingness to engage within twenty-four hours of learning of the opportunity, and deal talking on Friday night all signaled seriousness of purpose.

We had the attention of the right audience. We were talking with *the* respective decision-makers.

All day Saturday and Saturday night past midnight were equally intense. In multi-hour phone conferences Goliath #1 indicated they wanted to participate in the auction, but required some sensitive information we weren't eager to provide. They explained that after receipt, they would provide an indication of interest on Monday.

That's fast and aggressive, but their competitor was faster and more aggressive.

> **Goliath #2:** "We're going to buy Triad. How can we do that?"
>
> **Intermediary:** "Here's some information that may help.
>
> "I probably shouldn't tell you this, but we're hearing back from your competitor on Monday."
>
> **Goliath #2:** "We're willing to work non-stop through tonight and tomorrow.
>
> "Are you?"

A few hours later (2:00 a.m. on Sunday) Goliath #2 made an authentic offer at a specific price, and asked if we could meet with them later that day.

It was logistically impossible for everyone to meet in the same place on Sunday. Plane schedules and distance alone precluded that. The next best alternative was that six hours later (8:00 a.m.) everyone on the sell-side (CEO, CFO, Intermediary, team of lawyers) met in my office for a conference call with a matching buy-side team.

Sell-side DealCirclers all wanted to be in the same room so we:

- could *see* each other,
- *hand signal* if a conversation was going poorly,
- *pass notes* to re-direct how best to proceed or respond,
- *write* on a white board outlining different approaches in real time, and
- easily *step out* for smaller, more private meetings if necessary.

Our assumption was they were doing the same.

The counterparties talked for two hours and then mutually agreed to break for an hour recess so everyone could assess. Then we talked for another four hours before mutually agreeing to break.

When we resumed, Triad's CEO told Goliath #2's CEO that they were *"in the neighborhood"* of a preemptive offer, but would be escorted *"out of the neighborhood"* unless the purchase price was increased by 20%.

A high level of playing chicken. Would they increase their price or walk from the deal?

We broke for an "hour." No re-engagement. As every additional second passed after the one hour mark (and nearing the *two* hour mark), the whole Seller side was progressively jumpier. Not our CEO. He was totally confident.

When they called back, Goliath #2 simply said, *"You've* got your price and *we've* got this deal."

This was staged theater plus nicely improvised music. We

- set the *stage,*
- cast the *narrator,*
- chose the *lead actors,*
- wrote the *plot line and negotiating script,*
- set a super-fast *tempo,*
- conducted the deal from *overture to final curtain,* and
- got a *standing ovation* from the only audience we cared about: us!

As Shakespeare might have said if he were a business bard, "All's Well That Ends Well."

This transaction was a highly intentional Big Bang. We didn't have to create scarcity because it was authentic. Our strategic planning challenge was more narrow; how to best frame and present the scarcity that each bidder already acknowledged.

Which of the following completely accurate statements would have triggered stronger emotions and moved you to bid more if you were the buyer? Triad is,

- One of 16 non-public competitors,
- One of *only* 16 non-public competitors,
- The *largest private* company in the industry,
- Triple the size of any other tuck-in, or
- 40% of the market the Goliath Duopoly doesn't own.

All analytically sound. All evoke different emotional responses. We identified the wheeling and dealing prism most beneficial to us, and relentlessly riveted the spotlight there. Scarcity was the undisputed star of the Triad show.

We've seen again (and again and again) how scarcity is near-universally critical to negotiation and sales triumphs. Maybe in the next chapter we should concentrate exclusively on this hyper-important concept.

Chapter 14 Key Takeaways

- Seller's maximize price in a controlled, staged auction,

    - run by an experienced intermediary,

    - directed only to financially capable buyers, and

    - resulting in at least two (but preferably three or more) bidders.

- Four important negotiation levers maximize emotional and financial pressure on bidders and favor sellers:

    - Time pressure,

    - Scarcity,

    - Competition, and

    - Fear of missing out.

- Can buyers disrupt the auction tactic? Only by dramatically and materially altering the *process* or *price*. Small, incremental changes accomplish nothing.

Buyers can distinguish themselves by offering unmatchable *certainty and speed to Closing*. No financing contingencies, no approvals needed (inside or outside the company), and minimal diligence. Available this week and only this week.

Separation can also be achieved by offering a *preemptive* purchase price as incentive. (You'll know it when you see it.) A price so high that Seller immediately accepts the offer and stops the auction, fearful of giving bidder time to change their mind, withdraw their offer, or walk away.

SCARCITY SELLS ... EVERYTHING

Why does a single word, a single selling and negotiating tactic, merit a single (noticeably short) chapter?

Scarcity sells *everything*. Startups. Private placements. Salad spinners. Ginsu knives. Companies.

Whether selling preferred stock or a company, always lead with emotion and close with analysis.

Working with Bob Hurwitz drove that point home and simultaneously accelerated the focus (as well as range) of my negotiating techniques. He was (and is) a master negotiator. Smart, funny, creative, and audacious. Bob understands human beings as they *are* (with all their fun, flaws, and foibles) and not how he might wish them to be.

Long before there's an exit, there was an origin story. Those businesses were at one time early-stage, high-risk startups. They raised capital by selling a vision of their future either to high net worth individuals or venture funds, rarely an even blend of the two.

Individual investors (Angels) *are* individuals; they tend to function like David. Venture funds are more institutional; they tend to function more like Goliath.

The dialogue below synthesizes numerous conversations and investor encounters from all over the planet, and from all sides of this type of transaction.

An entrepreneur (a budding Dealjammer) raising early capital either:

- *announces* quantitative scarcity (because those are the facts), or

- *creates* product or time scarcity (because scarcity is useful).

Entrepreneur: "We're raising $5 million and already have $4.6 million 'soft circled' (i.e., informally committed). Probably close early next week.

"Given how risky this enterprise is, it's surprising how quickly people have committed."

What is entrepreneur *really* saying?

- Smart people have already concluded the rewards outweigh risks. *Better hurry.*

- There's only $400,000 of stock left to buy. *Better hurry.*

- The deal is 90% sold out. Only 10% left. *Better hurry.*

Themes and variations on a theme.

Ask yourself how hard a commitment has to be before most entrepreneurs characterize a sale as soft-circled?

Entrepreneurs tend to be "hallucinogenically" optimistic. They want to believe they've made a sale, so they honestly believe they've made it.

What *I* heard as a polite brushoff ("Really interesting. I'll talk with my advisors about possibly buying $200,000") *they* heard as closing the sale ("I'm definitely buying $200,000 but have to go through a charade with my advisors, so I won't be second-guessed by them later").

I saw investor avoidance behavior (don't want to say "no"). *They saw* investor acceptance behavior ("yes," but with some irrelevant hoops to jump through).

Were we at the same meeting?

My follow-up would be figuring out if there were any way to persuade this investor to invest. *Their* follow-up is to add $200,000 to the soft circle list.

On a subsequent phone call, entrepreneurs more bluntly pile on to this theme.

> **Entrepreneur**
> (to investor):
> "If you don't act *now*, there won't be anything left. You'll miss out on this once-in-a-lifetime, high-risk, higher-reward investment opportunity."

Once-in-a-lifetime epitomizes product and time scarcity. There's only a finite amount of this investment available, and only a finite time to invest. Scarcity has been *created* (more than identified) triggering greed and fear of missing out.

Reverse psychology is once again introduced to the negotiating cauldron.

> **Entrepreneur:**
> "Don't make a hasty decision. Didn't your mother tell you not to jump off a bridge just because other people are jumping?
>
> "Doesn't mean *you* should."

Everybody wants what they can't have and isn't available. The more you encourage prudence, the faster people demand to invest and abandon caution. This approach isn't limited to corporate finance; it works equally well selling commercial products.

How many late-night commercials hawk a product "exclusively" on TV? "You can't buy this in any store anywhere and this offer expires after the next five minutes."

Analytically this shouldn't be effective.

And yet, and yet, and yet … sales pitches provoking fear, greed, and scarcity continue hour-after-hour and day-after-day because they *are* effective. Retailers run going-out-of-business sales for decades. (Doesn't that seem like an excellent way to *stay* in business?)

The combination of scarcity with reverse psychology is a timeless sales, negotiating, and transactional aphrodisiac.

Circling back to corporate finance land, my investor group was evaluating buying some "restricted stock" (i.e., not registered with the SEC) directly from the founder of a microcap public company. (Stock like this is less valuable than SEC-registered stock.) He was a colorful, serial entrepreneur who had taken other companies public before and exited successfully.

Because meaningful blocks of stock like this aren't freely tradeable in thinly traded public marketplaces, they're customarily sold to investors at substantially below the currently quoted trading prices. If we ever wanted to sell this stock, there would be more supply from us than demand from the market. The price would plummet. (Adam Smith continues to speak to us.)

Our lead investor told Founder we were skeptical about the company as well as the stock price. (What went unspoken was how skeptical we were about him and his super slick sales presentation to us.)

Unfazed he instantaneously manufactured value and created scarcity as he responded with a deep Southern drawl:

Entrepreneur: "This is my only stock Ah'm ever selling. Just need some cash to build the mountain home in Aspen Ah been waitin' on.

"This here's what Ah call a 50-50 stock. It's either going to be worth 50 dollars or 50 cents."

He might have *talked* slow, but he didn't *think* slow.

And yet, and yet, and yet … with all our investment sophistication, intellectual reservations, and analytical skepticism, emotion drove us to buy his stock. To our chagrin, both his price predictions turned out to be too high. No one's easier to sell than a salesman.

Chapter 15 Key Takeaways

Whether you're raising money or selling a business, make the sale with emotion and close with logic and analysis.

- Everyone wants to invest in the over-subscribed equity raise or buy the business someone else is about to buy. People value what they can't have and isn't available. Fear of missing out invokes a curious mix of fear and greed.

    - *Greed*, because if everyone else bought something, that's proof that whatever it is must be good and valuable.

    - *Fear*, because I'll feel bad, stupid, embarrassed, or unhappy if I missed a profitable opportunity I could have taken.

- Dealjammers either *identify* scarcity (because it's real), or portray and convey facts to *create* scarcity (because that's useful).

Scarcity sells everything.

Framing is fine, and to be encouraged. Lying is not. There's an important difference between persuasion and a Ponzi scheme.

CHAPTER 16

HUMOR AND ANGER; NEGOTIATING'S YIN AND YANG

Self-deprecatory humor is (hopefully) sprinkled throughout this book, just as it has been with every deal I've taken part in. You can't laugh at yourself enough, let alone too much. (In my case there's a *lot* of material to work with!)

When people laugh *with* you in a negotiation they're less inclined to get angry *at* you or argue as hard as they otherwise might. Humor is a social lubricant helping to create DealGlue and Sustainable Deal Empathy.

It's comical. It's practical. It's tactical.

The whole page has to go?

If you designate *everything* as a crisis or a "deal killer" then fairly soon *nothing* is a crisis or a deal killer. Save your bullets for when you need them. Overuse degrades and diminishes their utility.

Flash back to *Aesop's Fables* and the gruesome fate of the boy who falsely cried wolf twice.

When you *do* tell the truth (something legitimately is a dealbreaker for you) no one will believe you.

Dealjammers don't say something is a "deal killer" unless that's categorically true. A hollow threat is worse than no threat at all. (We'll come back to this).

About twenty minutes and (twenty-nine pages) into negotiating the reps and warranties section of definitive acquisition documents, this exchange occurred.

Hyperbolic sell-side counterparty:	"This *whole page* has got to go. This is terrible/outrageous/unacceptable."
Me:	"Really? The whole page?"
Hyperbolic Counterparty:	"Yes."
Me (pointing to bottom of page):	"How about this down here?" *Group laughter.*
Hyperbolic Counterparty:	"Marc, don't be ridiculous. That's the *page number.*"
Me:	"I know. But it's on the page so I wanted to make sure."
Me (pointing to the *middle* of the page):	"How about this sentence here?" *Group laughter.*
Hyperbolic Counterparty:	"No, that's not a problem."
Me:	"And *this* sentence here at the top?"
***Decreasingly* Hyperbolic Counterparty:**	"Yeah, that's OK too."

> **Me:** "I'm having some focus issues here. What exactly on this page really *is* a problem for you?"

> **De-Hyperboliced Counterparty:** "It's these three words right here."

> **Me:** "OK. Let's address them."

When I'm really angry, I *lower* my voice, simultaneously adding "steel" to my tone. Total control. Everyone has to lean toward me to hear. I own the room. That's essentially what happened in the driveway meeting with Money Investor's Angry Leader by establishing a calm but urgent atmosphere to decide the fate of Ruth's Retail.

You can't use stronger adjectives to express stronger feelings if you've already said that everything is "*disgraceful, outrageous, fake, and totally unacceptable.*" Ultimately the hyperbolic, endlessly aggressive style is self-limiting and self-defeating.

Anger's only useful when it's useful.

Anger is the opposite of (but complementary to) humor.

Sometimes responding with anger or yelling *is* appropriate. When? It's most effective if it's outside the boundaries of your normal negotiating behavior.

If your customary tone of voice is 50-60 decibels (normal speaking volume) and you escalate to 70 decibels (loud TV or stereo), you'll get most people's attention. If you *further* escalate to 80 decibels (aircraft takeoff) *everyone* will pay attention because of the startling contrast.

If every word from your mouth is aggressive and loud (starting at 75 decibels) what variation can you introduce to emphasize a point? 125 decibels? A rocket ship taking off?

The only humans (and I use that term lightly) who more often than not generate that painful level of noise are bad DJs at a teenage party with an over-burdened, inadequate sound system.

If you yell continuously, and everything is a deal breaker, there's nowhere to go. You've boxed yourself in. The airplane already took off.

That approach communicates that you think you're Goliath and you have Goliath's leverage (whether you do or you don't). You're trying to invoke the deal world's golden rule: "She who has the gold makes the rules."

Simplifies deal-making considerably. It's Goliath's way or the highway.

You may be the rare person who has, believes, or *acts* as if they have the upper hand and leverage in every set of circumstances. This may be founded on a sizable net worth, social status, or purely on self-delusion. Being a bully may consistently work very well for you.

If it does, don't even think about changing your style to become a better negotiator. Empathy is probably *not* in your DNA and you can't fake it. If it ain't broke, don't fix it.

But make sure you have the power advantage and all the leverage in every transaction you are involved in. If you don't, everyone will remember who you are, and you'll pay a steep price of retribution in subtle and unsubtle ways.

You may want to change your style if you want a better epitaph or improving your chances of getting into heaven. Neither is bad motivation.

We all encounter folks whose unremitting style is acting like Goliath, making every issue (large or small) a confrontation, a deal-breaker, or both.

They may make an occasional spectacularly good deal. Some counterparties will "give up" emotionally and agree to every confrontational demand. Goliath-types trumpet those "victories."

I am caveman, hear me roar.

Those wins will be more than offset over time by their *losses,* good deals they needlessly killed, not to mention deals they'll never see because their unattractive reputation proceeds them.

Many potential counterparties will be turned off by relentless fighting. They'll withdraw from aversive negotiation rather than further engage. Definitely not the way to convert a *willing* seller to a *motivated* seller.

By insisting there's only one way to do something (i.e., *their* way) they preclude viable alternatives that would have accommodated both counterparties and led to a desirable deal. Not only won't Goliath-types explore different paths, they may not even *recognize* their existence.

How can those of us who aren't Goliath respond to Goliath?

The first time a counterparty uses the word "dealbreaker" my reaction tends to be non-committal, something akin to "duly noted." Acknowledging (but not engaging with) the threat.

Individuals like that tend to repeat themselves, they're a one-trick pony. (By the way, *not* the pony we're looking for). Their only tool is a jackhammer so every problem must be a nail.

After they've made the same threat repeatedly (and I assure you they will), I *do* engage, pleasantly saying,

> **Me** (very calmly, 60 decibels tops): "Am I right that's the 15th business issue you've identified as a 'dealbreaker'? That's not going to happen.
>
> "Should we stop now and save us both aggravation, or would you rather re-set this conversation and consider how we might get a deal done?"

Always nice to give people a choice. What are their options?

- Laugh it off as if the term "dealbreaker" doesn't really *mean* dealbreaker. "It's just a figure of speech. Sorry if you misconstrued."
- Narrow their fifteen enunciated dealbreakers to a single, real dealbreaker … if there is one.
- Start with a different perspective and genuinely try to make a deal now that they know you won't be bullied.

Bullies tend to be insecure cowards. If you shove back, they back down and change their tune. If you don't, they won't.

Dealjammer secret

Sometimes the anger you're dealing with comes from your counterparty. Sometimes it comes from *yourself.* Stuff happens. If you're a human being, you can't always control your emotions when someone's totally obnoxious or insulting. (Or at least I can't.)

We were in Des Moines working with a highly problematic Seller. They thought they were supersmart and super tough. Not my assessment. Despite my own rule to never let myself get angry in a business negotiation (unless I choose to), they had punched my buttons one too many times.

> **Me:** "I'm going to take a break now. This discussion isn't headed to a particularly good place. If I say anything now, we'll probably all regret it. I'm taking a walk."

I *didn't* ask permission to leave. I *announced* it.

I *didn't* say, I'll be back in *five* minutes, or *ten* minutes, or *twenty* minutes.

Simply, "I'm taking a walk."

I clearly communicated my anger. Very, *very* angry. Easy. This wasn't *pretending* to be angry. I was *really* honked off.

Leaving the meeting gave *me* time to cool off and think. Leaving the meeting gave my *counterparty* time to cool off and think.

Not specifying when (or if) I'd be back increased the ambiguity and Seller's tension. Here's my hypothesis of what happened in my absence.

> **Seller:** "He seems *boiling.* Do you think he's so furious we just broke the deal? Maybe we should back off from our last proposal.
>
> "What should we do if he comes back?"

On returning (after walking around the block) I did my best Martin Sheen-as-President Bartlett imitation from the *West Wing*.

> **Me:** "Well, that went well. Don't you think?"
>
> *Nervous laughter.*
>
> **Me:** "Where should we pick up our *discussion*?"

Seller promptly made an overtly conciliatory remark in conversational tones (55 decibels). Heat in the room went down tremendously. Civil dialogue; not Civil War.

How to say "Deal Killer" like a Deal*jammer*

I wish it were otherwise, but occasionally something authentically *is* a deal killer. Take a short trip down memory lane to Tiger Tights and the Reluctant Spouse who couldn't surrender her Family name.

Never make a threat unless you're prepared to carry it out. You can only say something is a deal killer *once*. If you don't follow through, you've lost all your negotiating credibility.

All of this is epitomized by a comment my Dad made to me when I was too young to understand.

> **Dad:** "Never pull a gun unless you're prepared to shoot."

A little militaristic for my taste but accurate.

It's happened more than once that a counterparty literally asked me if something was a deal killer (almost begging me to say that it was). There was nothing to be gained by responding head-on.

> **Counterparty:** "Are you saying this is a deal killer?"
>
> **Me:** "From everything I already knew before this meeting (and have confirmed by observation) you're a really smart guy. You understand our common goal is to get a deal done.

> "So I'm comfortable relying on your en-
> lightened self-interest to answer your
> own question."

I could have answered "*Yes*, this *is* a deal killer."

That's a challenge. Mine was a compliment.

Which is more likely to give him emotional space to back off without feeling like he was being forced to back off? The Proverbial
soft answer.

No one likes to be told "no"—not a child by a parent, not a student
by a teacher, and not a counterparty by their counterparty. You'll
deal with less intransigent anger if you don't create it.

"No" can be a complete, one-word sentence like John Wayne's
"Nope." You can also say "no" using other nuanced alternatives.
Dealjammers cast a wide net searching for more ways to say "no"
without saying "no" (or "nope" without saying "nope").

Here are four ways I've given iron-willed negative responses without using the words "no" or "dealbreaker."

> **Me:**   #1. "I have flexibility on some issues, but
> this isn't one of them."
>
> #2. "Let me think about that; maybe we
> can reconsider later."
>
> #3. "I hate this provision when I'm on
> your side of the table, but it's what we have
> to have on this side. I'm sympathetic but
> not capable of yielding."
>
> #4. "*I'd* be completely OK with that, *but* it
> can't be agreed to unless our irrational and
> unreasonable CEO who's on vacation for
> the next three months specifically tells me
> 'yes,' in person, face-to-face, in his office."

Here's how one of my favorite counterparties *bellowed* "no" without exceeding 60 decibels. At judiciously chosen moments his pre-
cise words were:

<table>
<tr><td>Favorite counterparty to me:</td><td>"That's just a non-starter. Marc, that's just a non-starter. You know what I mean? That's just a non-starter."</td></tr>
</table>

Awesome use of repetitive rhythm to drum home his statement.

He said it earnestly, powerfully, and only when true. He never postured. His credibility was high. Two things then typically happened:

- I started laughing, and

- I stopped asking.

My equivalent?

<table>
<tr><td>Me:</td><td>"If you're wondering, what you're looking at isn't a window of opportunity, it's a wall."</td></tr>
</table>

Those are six unequivocal "no's" without unnecessarily enraging your counterparty.

Even the harshest, most rigid response can be framed so it's difficult for your counterparty to get angry let alone repeat their same request.

How to say "deal killer" like a "deal *killer*"

If you're trying to say "no," infuriate your counterparty, and kill the deal at the same time, it's not hard. *Don't* frame your "no." Announce without explanation (as if it's self-evident to anyone over the age of seven) that their request can't be accommodated because "it's against company policy."

Pronounce that as if the company's view is sacred. Almost blasphemous that your counterparty had the temerity to even raise the subject.

Alternatives?

Assuming you're not bluffing (and there really *is* a policy) explain *what* the policy is, *what* it accomplishes for the company, and *why* they have it. Don't run away from articulating your own self-interest.

In a perfect world your explanation is so convincing that no one could disagree. Acceptance would be instantaneous.

Limitations to this approach?

To be believable, you actually need to know why the clause/provision/representation exists and why it's truly unchangeable. Show-stopping answers include:

Negotiator: #1. "I'm sorry but *government* regulations require it."

#2. "We're a *global company*. We sign standard documents like this around the world hundreds of times per day. They can't be subject to one-off negotiation."

#3. "Our *insurance policy* only covers us if these pre-approved words are used. No one except our General Counsel or Board can change them. Even *they* can only change them with the insurance carrier's permission."

Your counterparty may not *like* those responses, but they *likely will respect* them. Your "no" wasn't arbitrary or capricious.

Not many counterparties suppose they have the power (or the pocketbook) to negotiate with the government, a global company, or an insurance carrier.

Don Quixote aside, most people won't waste their time and emotion on fruitless forays.

Nonetheless you're at an impasse. You're both stuck. *You* didn't make the policy. *You* can't *change* the policy. *You're* as powerless on this issue as your counterparty.

Scores of company policies are nonsensical, totally one-sided, and self-serving. You may be better off sympathetically acknowledging the policy *isn't* reasonable. Don't insult your counterparty's intelligence by defending the indefensible. It makes you look foolish or worse.

Binary decision time. Yield the point. Walk away.

What if someone says deal killer and you don't *hear* it?

A company (we'll call them Down-and-Out) was in formal receivership in Canada (similar to a US bankruptcy court). Bad blood existed between the senior management teams of the distressed business and my client (Barracuda Buyer). It was helpful that all three of my client's senior executives (Executive Chairman, CEO, and President) were on a long-scheduled deep sea fishing trip and inaccessible.

Only my client's CFO and I were present at the negotiating table. We reached agreement with the Down-and-Outers on purchase price and payment method (cash plus debt forgiveness) and were deep in the weeds of definitive documents.

Great deal progress and momentum.

As a sign of good faith, we extended an olive branch of sorts to Seller's senior management by asking for only two years of indemnity for breach of Seller's reps and warranties.

In our corresponding US experience that indemnification period was favorable to Seller. In these troubled circumstances Buyer's diligence and self-protection is limited. Buyer's reliance on Seller's representations is higher than normal.

Seller's negotiator at the table was Francois, a partner in a Big 4 accounting firm in Canada. He kept saying, "No, it *cannot* be two years. The indemnity period must be limited to eight months."

This back-and-forth occurred multiple times. He repeated the same phrase with increasing passion and heat. I did the same because I didn't know any alternative way of framing ours.

Although I couldn't imitate the fabulous way a friend of mine furrows his brow and looks incredulous, I borrowed his effective approach.

Me:	"I'm *puzzled*. Is there a reason why you keep insisting on an eight-month indemnity period? Help me out here."
Francois (indignantly):	"Well *yes*."
Me:	"Are you willing to share?"
Francois:	"I'm a court-appointed *receiver*. Under Canadian law I'm financially protected while I'm under the Court's authority. I can't be sued personally. That authority expires eight months from now. After that I'd be personally liable for any Seller indemnity. I can't and won't do that."

Straightforward, easily understandable explanation. *Not* arbitrary or capricious. Would have been quite helpful if he'd volunteered this information earlier.

No glory in negotiating this point on his part. Little glory in ours.

We viewed him as an intermediary being needlessly stubborn in an area of the deal where he had no dog in the fight. I really *was* puzzled. Why was he fighting so hard? It wasn't his money. Was it?

Unlike the balance of the documents (where he was truly an *intermediary*), with respect to indemnity Francois was the *principal,* an economic stakeholder in this DealCircle with decision-making power. It *was* his money.

A generous interpretation would be he was trying (but failing) to politely articulate that this provision truly was a deal killer. We heard the literal words but not their message or implications.

From Francois' point of view? Our proposal was all risk, no reward.

In the world of acoustics and sound, the signal-to-noise ratio is the ratio of *relevant* information to *irrelevant* information. We misheard his repeated insistence as meaningless background noise to be ignored, not signal (meaningful primary input) to be closely paid attention to.

More-than-likely he assumed,

- we knew Canadian laws and nomenclature, and
- consequently our request was deranged and personally insulting.

I mean, we *looked* like we knew what we were doing. Ouch.

The request was dropped. Eight months agreed to. Part of Dealjamming is recognizing unalterable facts.

Accept those boundaries and terms, knowingly take that risk, or stop doing the deal.

Like most of us, Francois might have benefitted from coaching by my private banker. She was my all-time most useful instructor on the fine art of saying "no" or "deal killer" without saying "no." She *never* said "no" or turned me down. Here's an example of her velvet glove:

Me:	"A company I'm involved with needs a $5 million unsecured loan."
Banker (after checking with her Credit Committee):	"We'd be *delighted* to lend you $500,000.

"All we need is *your* personal guarantee *plus* the business maintaining at least $1 million in cash in their bank account with us." |

How could I be mad? The bank *wanted* to lend me money. They never said "no." They didn't turn me down. I turned them down.

Learning to say "no" is an artform worth mastering.

Lead with a smile. Doesn't cost you anything. If a deal breaks, *leave* with a smile. You never know if that moment is an ending or a beginning.

On that note, let's fix our gaze on how the Grateful Dead influenced Dealjamming.

Chapter 16 Key Takeaways

- Humor can gently puncture some pompous, arrogant, angry balloons and simultaneously create negotiating value.

People laughing *with* you (or even *at* you), are easier to interact with. Human bonds form, ears open, people hear you more easily.

- It's simple (not simplistic) that **people like to do business with people they like to do business with**. Treat others as you'd like to be treated. Don't over-think this.

- Avoid using the emotionally charged term "deal killer." If the phrase makes you cringe when you hear it, don't say it.

Find your own, uniquely best way to express that an issue is non-negotiable. The declaration is most effective if true, and buttressed by the words, phrase, and delivery conveying it.

Straight-forwardly articulate *why* you care about a contested issue, *how* it benefits you, and the importance you attach to it.

Be comfortable. Generally, it won't surprise your counterparty; it's what they already assumed.

But if it does startle them, the mutual education benefits both of you. You've given them a compelling reason to change their previous response, to yield on a point. To compromise without feeling compromised.

And vice versa. *Always* vice versa.

CHAPTER 17

THE GRATEFUL DEAD: AMERICA'S MUSICAL VENTURE CAPITALISTS

Let's share a few last stories and musings.

Robert Hunter (Jerry Garcia's lyricist) might have been talking about the Grateful Dead, Dealjammers, venture capital, or negotiating when he observed "Songwriting is 51% craft and 49% feel."

Garcia's observations are even more evocative and telling:

> *The nature of what we're doing is something, which by its very nature, is* non-formulaic *[emphasis added]. There's no way that you can make it happen by intention alone. It's something that you have to sort of allow it to happen, and you have to allow for it to happen.*

Negotiating deals is a similar curious mix of domain knowledge, intuition, fluidity, and real-time reaction. 51% craft; 49% feel. That's why deal *principles* are useful, but mechanical rules to be applied fall short.

Pragmatism governs.

In Grateful Dead-speak:

> *For us, it's mainly been the thing of what works … Things pop up and if they work you incorporate them, unconsciously almost. If they don't work, you discard them, almost equally unconsciously. If something doesn't work, it becomes obvious immediately. This just isn't going to work.*

Exploration is not commitment, and results aren't guaranteed.

The Grateful Dead explored musical opportunities from every possible angle. The song-as-written represented only the initial framework for "Musical Impressionism," not color by number. Their approach to music and jamming was vulnerable and risky.

The group didn't play or behave as if bounded by structure. They examined, tore down, and rebuilt every song's structure. Per Bob Weir, "The same song on a different day was a different song." And Garcia layered on top of that the view that "you can't repeat things because each time is different. The universe has changed. Everything has changed."

Grateful Dead's musical risks had the upside for enormous rewards. With those levels of risk sometimes the magic simply isn't going to work.

Not every Dealjam is gorgeous.

The corporate finance analogy and metaphor?

Venture capitalists invest money in early-stage, high-risk, high-reward companies. There is little certainty about how the business path forward will unfold or what the rewards will be.

Sometimes deal magic happens, the company is an extraordinary success, and venture investors win fifty times the amount of their investment.

Sometimes *anti-magic* happens. Investors lose 100% of their investment. In Las Vegas-lingo if you roll the dice enough times, you'll crap out more than once.

Every deal isn't gorgeous.

Sound familiar?

Lessons from the Golden Road, or "Shakedown Street"

Following a Grateful Dead concert, a few friends and I hung out with the band at their hotel. This conversation occurred:

Grateful Dead Bandmate:	"Marc, what did you think about the show tonight?"
Me:	"It confirmed my theory you guys are America's Musical Venture Capitalists."
Same Bandmate:	"Say what?"

The first set was probably the *worst* set I ever heard them play. On multiple occasions they simply stopped playing. Jams met dead ends. No shared musical momentum or direction.

A song you don't want to sing. A broken deal you don't want to make … at least not now.

The second set was probably the *best* set I ever heard them play. Flawless. From the opening chords energy flowed from the band to the audience and back again. A "musical flywheel." The music effortlessly ignited and soared.

Bob Weir describes it much better:

> *Sometimes it's a huge amble, where you're just on top of the lid, and it's not going anywhere, and sometimes you walk on the stage and from the first note, the afterburner kicks in.*

Some corporate finance takeaways?

There are lots of *different* deals within each imaginable deal, just as there are lots of different songs within each song. They're different, not necessarily better or worse. Many are worthwhile. Many are not.

There isn't a single pre-ordained paradigm, rarely a unique deal that's *perfect* while no other configurations are worth doing.

Good, bad, or ugly deals and jams are best measured in the *aggregate* (the mosaic of terms and totality of the risk-reward ratio).

Some possible configurations are,

- *flat-out spectacular* deals for *both* parties,

- *good enough* that they're worth doing, or

- *flat-out terrible* and should be avoided. Stop the jam. Kill the deal.

Close the *spectacular* ones, use discretion on the *good enough* ones, and run (don't walk) away from the *terrible* ones. That's what smart Dealjammers do.

Recommended background music for your inner ear is Kenny Rogers singing "The Gambler." Sometimes staying in the game is smart. Sometimes not so much. Hone your instincts and then trust them.

There are no rules in a Deal or a Jam or a Knife Fight.

Moving from the Grateful Dead's expansive view of songs to our imaginary negotiating conference table, it's not surprising the first structural rule remains "there are no rules." The second structural rule is "there are no rules in a Deal or a Jam or a Knife Fight."

The insight that there are no absolute rules doesn't imply there aren't some *skills* and *guidance* for Dealjammers.

Buyer's lawyer (in tones dripping with condescension): "Four years for the Escrow period is *market*."

Implication in lawyer-speak?

Any lawyer who doesn't know this rule is an idiot; at a minimum they should be disbarred.

Me: "With due respect, there's no such thing as '*market*.' Even if there were I don't feel bound by it. You're buying this company from *me*, not the *market*. Or you're not.

"What I agree to *is* the new market."

Buyer's lawyer   "Every deal I've done has had a four-year
(unabashed):   Escrow period."

Me (sweetly   "Wow. Surprised you've done so few deals.
and gently   We're good with eighteen months."
but arguably a
little snarkily):

An ending Dealjamming observation made by science fiction writ-er John Wyndham in *Re-Birth* (and later echoed by Bay Area band Jefferson Airplane): "… life is change, that is how it differs from the rocks, change is its very nature."

I never wanted to be a rock. Did you?

All the rest is commentary.

Chapter 17 Key Takeaways

- You have to master your craft's domain substance before performing well in *any arena*; basketball, music, or deals. Knowledge opens you up to possibility, implication, and intuition.

Deviations from the norm can't happen if artists (players, jam bands, or Dealjammers) don't *know* the norm, the script as written.

There's much to understand about deals. There's even more to learn about people.

- The Grateful Dead's high-risk willingness to play "Bertha" for three minutes one night and thirty-two minutes the next prompted my observation that *"Structure unexamined is Stricture."* They never stopped re-imagining the unknowns in a song.

Some sets were terrible.

If you put your head in the lion's mouth enough times, eventually the lion wins.

Those musical jaunts may not have succeeded but they equally didn't fail.

Exploration is not commitment.

Most jams were transcendent. Risks taken were exceeded by rewards reaped. Music and audience gelled, and their "Deal" came together. Musical venture capitalists on a tightrope *"Without a Net."*

- We can't all be the best at what we do, neither Dealjammers nor the Grateful Dead. We can all *strive* to be Dealjammers and the best version of ourselves in what we do.

Forge your own set of principles (your own maxims). Synthesize the words or music of others. Every musician, every human, stands on the shoulders of those who came before us. Just don't stop there.

OUTRODUCTION

A swan song is the beautiful, legendary song sung only once by a swan as it's dying.

Instead of singing a final song of any color swan, here's the essence of what I've tried to share, presented as my *coda*.

Stories have enduring power to change the world, to change yourself.

They *inspire*, they *aspire*, they *illuminate*; they let you *ruminate*.

Stories expand the nation of your imagination and your power for innovation and negotiation.

They let you feel and reveal and seal the deal. You may see yourself as part of the past or all of the cast of each story or each allegory. It's all good.

We all yearn to learn but not through school teaching or preaching.

There are so many ways to be human.

Counterparties come in all ages, shapes, genders, hues, and sizes. You don't have to love them all but Dealjammer success comes most easily by understanding and respecting all.

They're the human clay you mold your deals from.

If you're an empathetic, engaged, and open listener, demonstrably willing to jam and open to responding, you'll recognize and see deal alternatives and commonalities more clearly and you'll hear better.

You'll become more human to your counterparties. Not their enemy. Not the other side. Not the *other*.

From my tiny place on a very large globe my working hypothesis is that approaching life and deals with humor, intellectual humility, and compassion may not be a bad thing. ***People like to do business with people they like to do business with.***

Draw your own inferences from these stories. See what *you* think about trusting the power of music and magic, myth and metaphor, and (with context and color commentary) Morgenstern's Maxims.

Thanks for listening.

MHM

THE DEALCIRCLE

Concentric circles of visible and invisible negotiation stakeholders today (Closing) and tomorrow (Future)

Visible Stakeholders

Invisible Stakeholders

INDEX TO MORGENSTERN'S MAXIMS

(IN ORDER OF APPEARANCE)

The obvious isn't always optimal, and the optimal isn't always obvious. 179

A body not in motion trends toward falling apart. 192

Speed is a tactic. Speed is a strategy. 192

God gave you one mouth and two ears; the ratio wasn't an accident. 193

Dealjammers can compromise without feeling compromised. 204

Emails don't create dialogue; they create sequential monologue. 204

Maximize your optionalities. 209

If you put your head in the lion's mouth enough times, eventually the lion wins. 217

I'd rather own some percentage of something than 100% of nothing. 219

What matters about capital isn't price, it's availability. 219

If you volunteer to be a hostage, prepare to pay ransom. 224

If you put your head in the mouths of enough lions, enough times, the lions win. 224

Scarcity sells everything. 245

Anger's only useful when it's useful. 253

People like to do business with people they like to do business with. 264

Exploration is not commitment, and results aren't guaranteed. 265

There are no rules in a Deal or a Jam or a Knife Fight. 268

There are so many ways to be human. 271

ACKNOWLEDGMENTS

No one springs fully borne from the loins of Zeus. I've had exceptional mentors, co-investors, co-founders, family, clients, and law partners and benefitted from all in growing, managing, financing, and selling businesses.

My Senior Partner (Bennett Yanowitz) taught me, challenged me, supported me, and invested with me for almost thirty fun-filled years.

Bob Hurwitz's joy for life, people, and deals has made collaborating with him for forty years a non-stop delight.

Some deal savvy beta readers, entrepreneurs, and friends thoughtfully read portions of earlier drafts of this book and offered useful comments and badly needed encouragement.

They included Paul Clark, Ron DeGrandis, Tyler Dikman, Jeremy Fiance, Chris Formant, Ann Georgi, Vikas Khanna, Tim Mueller, Scott Roulston, David Meerman Scott, and Joel Yanowitz.

A dedicated handful persevered over several years, read multiple versions, and repeatedly provided penetrating insights and feedback palpably shaping the final outcome: Ryan Alshak, Kira Bellocq, Matt Chanoff, Jared Hyatt, Danielle Lackey, Randy Markey, Steve Oesterle, and my best friend, Danny Wolpaw. I am deeply indebted to them.

My long-time Executive Assistant (Terri Yursky) worked early and late, nights and weekends, with patience, competence, and unflagging good humor.

Unrelenting (but loving and valuable) criticism and guidance also came from my son (David), son-in-law (Raphi), and daughter

(Sarah). My one-year old grandson (Simon Gabriel Morgen-stern) provided unadulterated bliss, laughter, and inspiration but no advice.

My life collaborator and incomparable wife, Amy, stands alone for her probing questions and observations, emotional capital and intelligence, flexibility, faith, and support. She's the infrastructure this book is built on.